SpringerBriefs in Economics

More information about this series at http://www.springer.com/series/8876

Yoko Iwasaki

Industrial Organization in Iran

The Weakly Organized System of the Iranian Apparel Industry

Springer

Yoko Iwasaki
IDE-JETRO
Chiba
Japan

ISSN 2191-5504 ISSN 2191-5512 (electronic)
SpringerBriefs in Economics
ISBN 978-981-10-4578-3 ISBN 978-981-10-4579-0 (eBook)
DOI 10.1007/978-981-10-4579-0

Library of Congress Control Number: 2017937701

Printed on acid-free paper

This Springer imprint is published by Springer Nature
The registered company is Springer Nature Singapore Pte Ltd.
The registered company address is: 152 Beach Road, #21-01/04 Gateway East, Singapore 189721, Singapore

Preface

This book is based on various studies concerning Iran's textile and apparel industries published by the author since 1993. Through this work, I aim to inquire into the characteristics of the state of Iran's industrial organization.

I started fieldwork in Tehran in 1994, having already set about an investigation on the history and the present conditions of Iran's textile industry through the use of related literature. I was sent to Tehran by the Institute of Developing Economies as a Junior Overseas Researcher in February 1994, and this led me to make acquaintances in the local textile companies and develop an interest in the more concrete production and distribution system of Iranian firms. I started by interviewing textile firms as well as the brokers who worked with local Japanese companies, gradually adding Iranian apparel firms to my list of interviewees.

It is needless to say that Iran is blessed with abundant mineral resources including oil and gas. If you look at the breakdown of Iran's GDP, however, it is clear that the Iranian economy does not solely depend on these resources but has a comparatively well-balanced industrial structure comprising agriculture, manufacturing, and services. To gain a deep understanding of the Iranian economy, it is useful to look at the textile and apparel industries, which possess a long history and greater employment compared with the capital-intensive public sector of oil and gas. We can grasp the specific state of the Iranian people's labor and livelihood in these industries by investigating how they conduct their daily business and cope with problems.

My fieldwork revealed that the majority of Iran's apparel firms are very small in scale, lacking in capital integration or grouping observed, with little subcontracting. Each small-scale firm is a completely independent business entity. In Tehran, numerous independent small-scale firms would conduct their production based on their own expectation and market assessment, and this led to the development of a distribution system where each firm would send its products to the market on its own. Such a self-reliant system functions at all stages from production to sales, under circumstances where related firms are by no means organized. Iran's apparel firms embody the features of the manufacturers in the country's private sector in terms of their minuteness, independence, and weak relation with distribution channels. They are significant objects of study.

As discussed in this book, a massive amount of foreign apparel goods entered the Iranian market in the 2000s. This was brought about by changes in the trade policies of the Iranian government and the expansion of competition and sales power on the supply side (such as the development of China's "Specialized Markets"). There is nothing odd about cheap foreign goods selling well under such conditions. However, a significant and noteworthy aspect is that this inherent state of Iran's industrial organization has been the cause of the surging inflow of foreign goods. This state of industrial organization embodies "independent" small-scale firms not organized under the umbrella of big companies and an elastic market structure in which producers can easily venture out and become distributors. Such entrepreneurial attitude places much importance on diversifying operations. The more direct and influential players that brought about the rapid change in the domestic market were those who had been running their own businesses in Iran's apparel manufacturing industry. This book pays special attention to the influence that the state of existing industrial organization exerts on Iran's economic performance from the aforementioned perspective.

The state of Iran's industrial organization seems rather chaotic to those of us familiar with small-scale firms working faithfully for larger companies, but such a disorderly condition strongly reflects the patterns of organizations and human relations in Iranian society. Such a state affects not only the production process of a specific industry but also the related distribution channels and, consequently, the entire market structure. In other words, it has a great influence on the way the country's economy functions, and it is, therefore, quite important to understand it as a whole.

I stayed in Tehran for a year during 1994–1995 and later on for 2 years during 2009–2011 to conduct research (I had learned Persian language in my student days). I also made annual visits, usually research trips lasting a few weeks each time (although I did not always focus only on the textile and apparel industries). Throughout the 20 years or so of fieldwork in Tehran, I became acquainted with many Iranian entrepreneurs and businessmen. I sometimes requested the relevant trade associations to introduce me to someone appropriate, but often, those whom I had met previously would introduce me to someone else in the same business. In Iran, where the organizational relationships among firms are weak and each worker's own personal network plays a more important role in business, research activity cannot be easily conducted without such person-to-person mediations. The publication of this book would not have been possible without the many open-hearted Iranian people who have a large circle of acquaintances in the textile and apparel business.

Special thanks go to Dr. J. M. Ja'farī, the Representative Director of Iran Torino and Ms. F. Asnāfī, the then Manager of International Affairs of the Association of Iran Textile Industries, and Dr. S. A. Moujānī, an erudite scholar and my old friend. They have always been very helpful in introducing me to many creative and powerful Iranian entrepreneurs with all their useful contacts. Mr. M. Yektā, the then

Secretary of the Iran Textile Exporters' Association, was a reliable contractor who took on the difficult task of implementing my questionnaire survey. I would like to express my deep gratitude to the four of them and to all other Iranian collaborators and sources.

I also wish to convey my heartfelt thanks to Dr. S. ʻĀmelī, the then Dean of the Faculty of World Studies, University of Tehran, for accepting me as a visiting researcher during 2009–2011 and to Prof. M. Naqīzāde for providing generous support and advice. The Questionnaire Survey on Apparel Firms in Iran 2010 would never have been implemented without their thoughtful assistance and support.

The aforementioned questionnaire survey, conducted in 2010, was a part of a joint research project during 2009–2010 involving the Institute of Developing Economies and the Office of Need-based Program for Area Studies, Middle East within Asia: Law and Economics, Hitotsubashi University. In conducting this joint project in Iran, we faced various technical and financial difficulties. I sincerely thank Prof. Emeritus Hiroshi Kato of Hitotsubashi University and Dr. Erina Iwasaki, Professor of Sophia University, for bringing about a quick and amicable settlement to these issues.

All the research projects I conducted in Tehran that provide essential experimental data for this study have been sponsored by the Institute of Developing Economies.

I hope this book will be a small contribution to the study of the Iranian economy and to the understanding of Iran in a broader sense.

Chiba, Japan
February 2017

Yoko Iwasaki

Contents

About the Author

Yoko Iwasaki is a senior research fellow at the Institute of Developing Economies, Japan External Trade Organization. She received her Ph.D. in Economics from Hitotsubashi University in Tokyo, Japan. Her main research interests are economic institutions, economic behavior, and economic history in Iran. She has published several books and articles on the Iranian economy, including *Teheran shōbai ōrai: Iran shōnin no sekai* (*Doing business in Tehran: The customs and spirit of Iranian merchants*), 2004, IDE-JETRO.

Chapter 1
Introduction

Abstract Very small enterprises employing fewer than 10 workers make up the majority of firms in Iran's apparel-producing industry. Cooperation among firms has always been weak. A salient characteristic is that firms in the sector have shown a strong tendency to avoid involving themselves in the creation of vertical relationships between producers and distributors, unlike in Japan and other advanced industrialized countries. Following changes in government trade policy since the 2000s, these apparel firms are confronted with a massive inflow of Chinese-made clothing. It was occasionally reported that Iran's apparel market was being overwhelmed by Chinese products, but the reality is somewhat different. The study will discover real causes of this inflow, which not only reflect eminent price competitiveness and the supply capability of products of China's apparel industry but also the domestic state of production and distribution system of Iran's apparel industry.

Keywords Iran · Apparel industry · Small-scale firms · Inflow of Chinese products · Production and distribution system

In many cases of industrial production, related firms, and companies that participate in the manufacturing and distribution processes of a certain product are organized to a high degree.

Producers often create long-term and steady business relations with outside firms through procuring the necessary raw materials or making contract agreements. They also corral customers by building monopolistic distribution channels. On the other hand, distributors make an effort to secure punctual and credible producers from quality and price perspectives so that they can respond quickly to fickle consumer demand. If necessary, they invest in developing new products, enter into production, and lead the market.

Such business relations develop because firms try to minimize the stock risk (including that of intermediate stock) of best-selling products and to ensure a "stable and certain supply." To achieve the latter, they coordinate with related firms to eliminate uncertainties as far as possible. As a result, highly organized industrial systems exist in advanced industrialized countries like Japan. Arguments on "value

Y. Iwasaki, *Industrial Organization in Iran*, SpringerBriefs in Economics,
DOI 10.1007/978-981-10-4579-0_1

chain" or "supply chain" are based on such business relations that facilitate information sharing among firms, although the degrees of capital sharing or integration vary, to ensure that the entire manufacturing and merchandising process would be more efficient.

In the apparel industry in particular, distributors who are more informed of market trends have a strong tendency toward organizing producers. For example, in Japan, a type of firm called an "apparel manufacturing wholesaler (seizō-oroshi)" (see Chap. 4) who undertakes product planning and wholesale supply of the products, relies on a number of small sewing firms and their subcontractors entrusted with work. In the area where the small-scale firms gather, besides sewing firms, many tiny manufacturers like knitters and finishers have accumulated, which has led to the formation of an integrated production system through division of labor and cooperation (Arita 1978; Kurasawa 1995; Matsuo 1997; Iwasaki 2000; Kim and Abe 2002). In South Korea, merchants who have shops in the marketplace, known as Tōdai-mon Shijō, assume charge of planning and sales of the products while the small-scale firms agglomerated in the adjoining area receive contracts for production. It is well known as a producing center of apparel products and a massive wholesale market, and its production system reflects sales-related information directly and very quickly (Kim and Abe 2002).

Iran's apparel production scene, however, hardly displays such an organized system, as we will see in detail later. Information about merchandise and customers is never exchanged among those in charge of production and distribution; they integrate neither their businesses nor capital. It reveals an extremely peculiar condition in which firms never work together. If we compare this with the highly organized industrial systems present in advanced industrialized countries, the considerably less-organized state of Iran's apparel producers and distributors becomes more distinct.[1]

In the cases of Japan and South Korea, the immediate responses to markets that are indispensable to apparel production are realized by cooperation among firms. In Iran, by contrast, small-scale but independent apparel-producing firms and similarly independent distributors who seldom establish partnership with each other supply goods to the domestic markets of several classes, sharing little business information.

Very small enterprises employing fewer than 10 workers make up the majority of the firms operating in Iran's apparel-producing industry, a feature typical of the extremely small-scale nature of the industry as a whole. Iran is not home to any

[1]This kind of phenomenon, however, is not observed only in Iran. For example, in Vietnam where apparel production for export is thriving and high economic growth has recently been achieved, distributors do not necessarily lead the production activities so far as the production sector for the domestic market is concerned. It is reported that small producers supply low-priced goods entirely based on their own product planning (Gotō 2005). Also in China, which has now become a "world's factory," some small producers who are not integrated into a larger distribution channel operate independently around the "Specialized Market" (see Ding 2011; for more details, see Chap. 6). These cases make a good contrast to the apparel industries in Japan and South Korea, which developed almost from the beginning due to distributors' initiative (Arita 1978; Hanabusa 1978).

world-famous brand nor, with a few exceptions, is it an exporter of apparel. Most firms supply their products exclusively to the domestic market, and consequently Iran, unlike Turkey and some of the other Asian emergent countries, has never developed as a center of contracting work for foreign brands.

Nevertheless, the apparel industry has maintained a certain presence as a steady source of employment in Iran's manufacturing sector. This largely stems from the fact that for many years, the import of final consumption goods including apparel products was to a large extent restricted by the government as part of its declared policy of protecting domestic industries. Until the end of the 1990s, this restriction allowed Iran's apparel industry to monopolize internal demand without having to compete with foreign-made goods.

The Iranian government, however, relaxed its conventional restrictions on imports substantially from about 2002 onward. This resulted in massive amounts of foreign-made (mainly Chinese) apparel goods streaming into the domestic market. The volume of apparel imports as of 2005/06 (1384 in the Iranian calendar) was more than 200 times as much as in 1998/99 (1377) (Markaz-e Āmār-e Īrān 2000/01, 2001, 2002, 2003, 2004, 2005, 2006/07). Even the Japanese media became aware of the fact that a huge quantity of Chinese apparel goods was flowing into and inundating Iran's domestic market—see the Mainichi report remarking that "many Iranian textile manufacturers were driven into discontinuance of business."[2] Iran's apparel industry, which had been sheltered from international competition, was suddenly exposed to vigorous attack from an Asian newly industrializing country.

It has occasionally been reported that Iran's apparel market is overwhelmed by Chinese products, but the reality is somewhat different. Some small-scale firms formerly engaged solely in apparel production have recently ventured into buying and are bringing a huge quantity of apparel goods into the Iranian market from China's "Specialized Markets," which are sales centers of exportable manufactured commodities (see Chap. 6). In fact, those who do so are Iranian ex-producers that seem to be quick to seize new opportunities.

Why, in the case of Iran, has such a massive and rapid inflow of Chinese products occurred?

This study will examine the underlying reasons for this occurrence by focusing on the characteristics of Iranian industrial organization. In other words, we will analyze the characteristics that are the immediate causes of this situation. It goes without saying that the primary reason for this influx was the superior price competitiveness and the product supply capability of China's apparel industry. Later on in this book, we would also consider, as further conditions to the situation, the existence of a strong supplier along with the relaxation of import restrictions by the Iranian government at the time. Nevertheless, it is only natural that cheap foreign goods would sell well under such conditions. With more careful examination, however, we can discern the *structural* causes of the rapid inflow of foreign

[2]*Mainichi Shinbun*, September 17, 2004.

goods, which reflect the state of the domestic production and distribution system in Iran's apparel industry, as mentioned at the start of this chapter.

Most contributions to the existing literature on Iran's apparel industry, as exemplified by Shīrāzī (2010), use macroeconomic data to analyze the entire performance of this industry in terms of features such as output, profit rate, and amount of imports and exports. Unlike the present research, few studies have examined the ways in which the character of industrial organizations influences the whole industry's performance. In an attempt to make good this deficiency in the existing literature, this study clarifies the characteristics of the production and distribution system in Iran's textile and apparel industry using mainly the results of fieldwork carried out in Tehran.[3]

As will be explained in greater detail below, over the course of the research, a model emerged of the typical Iranian apparel firm that persists in maintaining independent operations regardless of its size, and which is inimical to the development of long-lasting business relations with other firms, let alone vertical integration between firms, in all stages from production to distribution. In other words, it is a distinguishing feature of Iran's apparel industry that the member firms are barely organized compared to their counterparts in advanced industrialized countries.

We will verify the proposition that the state of industrial organization in Iran's apparel industry is one of the key factors behind the rapid change in merchandise composition in the Iranian domestic market. This is especially so in the context of the emergence of enormous apparel production supply centers in China that have a policy of being "open to any purchaser" (Itō 2011). Through an investigation of the causal factors behind such a massive and rapid inflow of foreign (mainly Chinese) products into Iran, we seek to theorize how the nature of industrial organization and the entire system that they constitute can exert a great influence on the industry's competitiveness and resilience.

The remainder of the book is organized as follows. Chapter 2 provides a general overview of Iran's apparel industry's historical development. It follows its evolution from the modernization era until the present time. Chapter 3 details the typical pattern of apparel-producing firms in Iran and the well-known producing centers where the firms gather. Chapters 4 and 5 analyze in detail the conventional system of production and distribution in Iran's apparel industry and suggest how these industry characteristics help to explain the origins of the current changes. Chapter 6 focuses on the ways in which the system has changed under the new economic environment that emerged in the 2000s and investigates the actual impact of import liberalization on Iran's apparel industry. Chapter 7 concludes the discussion, showing how a type of globalization very different from the one pursued by the advanced countries was induced in Iran by the very state of the apparel industry's organization.

[3]For the detail of the results of fieldwork, see Iwasaki (1998), (2000), (2002), (2004), (2010), (2012a), (2012b).

References

Arita, T. (1978). Gifu Apareru Sangyō no Sanchi Kōzō to Kōzō Kaizen Seisaku (The Framework of Apparel Industrial Cluster in Gifu and the Structural Improvement Policies). *Meijō Shōgaku (Meijo Commercial Science), 27*(4), 83–127.

Ding, K. (2011). Chūgoku no Sangyō Hatten ni okeru Seisan, Ryūtsū Kankei:Sengyō Shijō Sisutemu no Shiten kara. (The relationship between production and distribution in the industrial development in China: From the viewpoint of specialized market system). http://www.ide.go.jp/Japanese/Publish/Download/Report/2010/pdf/2010_407_04.pdf

Gotō, K. (2005). Hōchimin-shi no Naiju muke Apareru Sangyō no Seisan to Ryūtsū Kōzō: Chien, Ketsuen Nettowāku no Kigyō kan Kankei to Shitauke Seisan. (The production and distribution structure of Ho Chi Minh City's domestic apparel industry: interfirm relationships of personal networks and subcontracting arrangements). *Ajia Keizai (Asian Economy), 46*(10), 2–25.

Hanabusa, Y. (1978). Kankoku Yushutsu Ifukugyō no Hatten Katei to Seichō Yōin. (South Korea's exporting garment industry: Its development and growth factors). *Ajia Keizai (Asian Economy), 19*(7), 15–32.

Itō, A. (2011). Chūgoku Zakka Sangyō Habu Giu no Kyōsōyūi to Inpakuto: Naze Kanojo wa Dobai o Nakanuki Shitanoka?"(Competitive Advantage and Impact of Yiwu, a Hub of Daily Goods Production in China). *Sedai Kōtaiki no Chūshō Kigyō Keiei. (Business Management of Small and Medium Enterprises in the period of the Generation Change)* (pp. 101–114). Tokyo: Dōyūkan.

Iwasaki, Y. (1998). The Role of the *Namāyande* in Iran's Textile Industry. *The Developing Economies, 36*(4), 440–458.

Iwasaki, Y. (2000). Iran no Seisan Soshiki to Ryūtsū kikō: Teheran Apareru Sangyō no Jirei. (The system of production and distribution in Iran: A Case Study of the Apparel Industry in Tehran). *Iran Kokumin Keizai no Dainamizumu. (The Dynamism of Iranian National Economy)* (pp. 93–129). Chiba: Institute of Developing Economies.

Iwasaki, Y. (2002). Teheran no Apareru Oroshiuri Shijō: Bonakudāru no Serinin Kinō. (The *Bonak-dār* as Auctioneer: A Case Study of Apparel Wholesale Market in Tehran). *Ajia Keizai (Asian Economy), 43*(2), 2–25.

Iwasaki, Y. (2004). *Teheran Shōbai Ōrai: Iran Shōnin no Sekai. (Doing business in Tehran: The customs and spirit of Iranian Merchants).* Chiba: Institute of Developing Economies.

Iwasaki, Y. (2010). *Questionnaire survey on apparel Firms in Iran 2010.* Middle East within Asia Research Report Series No. 11. Tokyo: Hitotsubashi University.

Iwasaki, Y. (2012a). The business management strategy of Iran's large apparel firms: Overview of results from a questionnaire survey and interviews 2009–2011. Discussion Paper No. 327. Chiba: Institute of Developing Economies.

Iwasaki, Y. (2012b). Globalization under a "low-organized" system: A case study on Iran's apparel industry. *Ajia Keizai (Asian Economy), 53*(5), 2–27.

Kim, R., & Abe, M. (2002). *Kankoku Tōdaimon Shijō no Hatten to Arata na Nikkan Apareru Sangyō Nettowāku no Keisei. (The development of Dongdaemun market in South Korea and new formation of apparel production networks between Japan and South Korea).* Chiba: Institute of Developing Economies.

Kurasawa, M. (1995). Ryūtsū no Tadankaisei to Henpinsei: Sen'i, Apareru Sangyō. (Multistep distribution system and returnable purchase: Textile and apparel industry). *Nihon no Ryūtsū (Distribution in Japan)* (pp. 189–223). Tokyo: University of Tokyo Press.

Markaz-e Āmār-e Īrān. (2000/01). *Sāl-nāme-ye Āmārī-ye Keshvar 1378 (Iran Statistical Yearbook)*, Tehrān.

Markaz-e Āmār-e Īrān. (2001). *Sāl-nāme-ye Āmārī-ye Keshvar 1379 (Iran Statistical Yearbook)*, Tehrān.

Markaz-e Āmār-e Īrān. (2002). *Sāl-nāme-ye Āmārī-ye Keshvar 1380 (Iran Statistical Yearbook)*, Tehrān.

Markaz-e Āmār-e Īrān (2003) *Sāl-nāme-ye Āmārī-ye Keshvar 1381 (Iran Statistical Yearbook)*, Tehrān.

Markaz-e Āmār-e Īrān. (2004). *Sāl-nāme-ye Āmārī-ye Keshvar 1382 (Iran Statistical Yearbook)*, Tehrān.

Markaz-e Āmār-e Īrān. (2005). *Sāl-nāme-ye Āmārī-ye Keshvar 1383 (Iran Statistical Yearbook)*, Tehrān.

Markaz-e Āmār-e Īrān. (2006/07). *Sāl-nāme-ye Āmārī-ye Keshvar 1384 (Iran Statistical Yearbook)*, Tehrān.

Matsuo, T. (1997). *Zukai Apareru Gyōkai Handobukku (Illustrative handbook of the apparel business)*. Tokyo: Tōyōkeizai-shinpōsha.

Shīrāzī, A. (2010). *Tahlīlī bar Toulīd va Tejārat-e Pūshāk dar Īrān. (An analysis on the cloth production and trading in Iran)*. Tehran: Sherkat-e Chāp o Nashr-e Bāzargānī.

Chapter 2
Outlook for Iran's Apparel Industry

Abstract The production and business environment for Iran's apparel industry as well as that for its parent textile industry was never quite stable. It had been ranked as the national mainstay industry from the modernization era through to oil nationalization as a way to realize import substitution. However, the government's industrialization strategy was de facto abandoned owing to the rapid growth in oil income. The restrictions and subsequent relaxations of textile and apparel imports were repeated in turn in response to changes in terms of trade arising from political circumstances. Meanwhile, strong demand backed by one of the biggest markets in the Middle East has continuously attracted private investment. Consequently, it never absolutely disappeared despite repeated rises and falls, and instead maintained a certain presence in Iran's manufacturing industries. It is rather noticeable that Iran's apparel industry has managed to supply products to the domestic market so far despite its minute scale under the aforementioned unstable business environment.

Keywords Industrialization strategy · Import substitution · Monopoly of foreign trade by the government · Import control system

2.1 Historical Development of the Textile and Apparel Industries and Their Business Environment

2.1.1 Modernization Era

Prior to discussing the industrial organization of contemporary Iran's apparel-producing industry, historical development process of the industry should be clarified.

The theme of industrialization has attracted significant interest from numerous countries around the world in twentieth century, particularly from Asian countries that were later to pursue economic development, where people became more motivated to achieve economic development, witnessing the economic prosperity of

Y. Iwasaki, *Industrial Organization in Iran*, SpringerBriefs in Economics,
DOI 10.1007/978-981-10-4579-0_2

the Western advanced industrialized countries; however, at the same time, these Asian countries were exposed to their menace. It was certainly an emergent task for them to realize the economic development through industrialization so that they could secure their political and economic independence.

Many countries threw their energy into development of a domestic textile industry, whose market potential seemed to be quite large, as an initial phase of modern industrialization. Iran was no exception to this rule. Manufacturing skills within Iran's textile products, typified in carpets and silk, had already attained a high level since early times and private capital had been invested briskly in the field. In the Qajar period, when modern industrialization had not yet begun on a full scale, Premier Amīr-e Kabīr, who was intent twentieth on protecting the existing domestic industries, conducted buildup policies for the textile industry, such as construction of a silk fabric factory and introducing a worker training system. These steps indicate that the textile industry was ranked as the mainstay industry for Iran during this period.

By the middle of the nineteenth century, Iran traded its various local specialties incessantly, such as Kermān's woolen fabrics, Isfahan's brocades, and the silk carpets of Yazd and Kāshān, with neighboring countries like India, Turkey, and Russia. It remained a textile exporting country, although it is pointed out that the industry had already begun to decline in those days. Circumstances changed, however, in the middle of the nineteenth century and imports of English textile products grew dramatically.

These changes resulted in changes to the composition of Iran's exports. Textile products, which had accounted for 25% of all Iran's export, were replaced by agricultural products such as fruits, rice, grain, and raw cotton. The only textile exports that increased were carpets, which accounted for 12% of all Iranian exports in 1913. The trading partners also changed from neighboring countries to European industrialized countries such as Britain and Russia (Issawi 1982, 17–43).

As mentioned earlier, the modernization of manufacturing industries became a critical issue in keen competition with Europe. However, it is thought that most of the domestic manufacturing sector maintained a traditional production system, with the few exceptions of modern spinning and weaving factories built in Tehran and Isfahan. Polak identified labor shortages, dishonest practices by managers, and high transportation costs for the introduction of machinery and equipment as the reasons why "factory production" in those days did not become established successfully in Iran (Issawi 1971, 275).

The establishment of the Pahlavi regime was a landmark for Iran's manufacturing industries—including the textile industry—from the viewpoint that the government pursued industrialization on its own initiative. The development strategy of Reza Shah, founder of the Pahlavi dynasty (1925–1941 on the throne), had a more comprehensive scheme compared with previous "modernization" policies.[1] That is, it included the modernization (Westernization, more precisely) of the political system through steps such as introducing a Western legal system, improving the tax collection system, and so on. It was partly a consequence of the Constitutional Revolution that took place at the beginning of the twentieth century. The government's industrialization policies were promoted as before, with public investment in Isfahan's textile industry listed first. Construction of the north–south railroad was also started in order to overcome deficiencies in transportation facilities, the biggest obstacle to Iran's industrial development.[2]

Policies from the Reza Shah era have some common characteristics that bear pointing out. First, the policies clearly intended to pursue "import substitution industrialization" which was adopted frequently at the first stage of industrialization by late-started countries. Many late-started countries promoted domestication of manufacturing products that they imported in order to prevent economic invasion by advanced industrialized countries. Support for the mainstay textile industry by Reza Shah clearly shows that Iran in those days sought to pursue this same strategy.[3]

Second, the government acquired the funds for industrialization through the old land-owing system (Gotō 2000).[4] Oil income had not yet become the government's effective revenue source, and its funds were severely limited. Therefore, the state played a key role in efficient collecting and redistribution of the domestic private funds scattered all over the country.

---

[1]The "modernization" policies pursued by Amīr-e Kabīr are well known as representative development attempts in nineteenth-century Iran, while the Qajar government was utterly unable to devise any appropriate measures to protect the domestic manufacturing sectors, which were still no more than the handcraft industry, from the harm caused by the inflow of cheap European manufactured commodities. According to Adamiyat, Amīr-e Kabīr recognized the importance of accomplishing Iran's own industrialization to prevent economic penetration by foreign countries. In those days, two sugar refinery mills, a spinning factory, a silk weaving factory and such were established with his encouragement, and European machinery was introduced. He also dispatched Iranian craftsmen to Russia and France for training. (Issawi 1971, 292–293) A series of his policies were rolled back after his dismissal in 1851. At this point of time, development issues were still raised, only against the inflow of European commodities, but now as a political issue and emergent treatment of symptoms toward the country's economic invasion by two great menaces, Russia and Britain.

[2]Railroad construction project began in 1927, and completed in 1938, connecting some routes that had already been in operation before the construction of traversing railroad. The route started from the Caspian Sea (Bandar-e Shāh) and ran through Tehran, Ahvāz to reach the Persian Gulf (Bandar-e Shāhpūr).

[3]Needless to say, the recovery of tariff autonomy in 1928 and the monopolization of foreign trade by the government, accompanied by 27 exclusive articles such as tobacco, sugar, and tea, played an important role.

[4]Gotō points out that the surplus from agricultural production in this period was invested in the public sector by the landholders who dwelled in cities through the banking system, and that the government's monopoly system of agricultural products sales supported the state finances.

The government's monopoly of foreign trade plainly indicates Iran's industrial protection policies during this period. Import–export businesses in Iran came to be completely under the government's control via the Law of Government's Monopoly in Foreign Trade (qānūn-e vā-gozārī-ye enhesār-e tejārat-e khārejī-ye mamlekat be doulat)[5] enacted in 1931. It stipulated that a foreign country's volume of exports to Iran must not be more than 20% of that country's volume of import from Iran. Furthermore, a 25–35% tariff was imposed on imported textile products (Bharier 1971, 178). This policy possibly intended to encourage industrial investment with the surplus private funds by excluding domestic merchants from the import–export business.

Refined sugar, matches, and cement factories were also prioritized by the government in addition to spinning and cotton weaving. The textile industry, which needed less initial investment and created mass employment, attracted more private funds. Although the precise conditions are unclear, according to Rabizade's record, twelve cotton spinning factories, five cotton weaving factories, six wool weaving factories, and a jute weaving factory were established in the form of joint-stock companies in 1932–38. The total capital was more than 190 million rial, which exceeded the total public investment at that time of 130 million rial. These factories employed approximately 15,000 workers, an amount almost double the public sector's employment (Rabizade 1975, 56). It is thought that relatively "large-scale factory" construction was promoted in those years.

It was reported, on the other hand, that many state-owned factories in the textile sector during the Reza Shah era were cotton spinning factories. This indicates that the government attempted to reduce imports through domestication of yarn production. By this move, a self-supply system would be established while the private sector took on the role of developing the remaining steps of the textile production, including final processing.

The Reza Shah era, as stated above, was the dawn of thorough industrialization for Iran, a period when the restructuring was aggressively conducted in the state's financial system although infrastructure was only partially developed and private industrial sector remained weak.

The level of domestic textile production in Iran at the time is unknown; however, raw cotton exports from Iran decreased by half within a decade after the end of the 1930s, according to international trade statistics (United Nations 1953, 170–173). One could surmise that the raw cotton that had been a conventional major export was instead allocated to domestic production. On the other hand, imports of cotton textile products, such as yarn, cotton fabric, and dyed cotton fabric, doubled in the same decade. Imports of synthetic fiber products, which had been low in 1930s, also increased considerably at the end of 1940s. These facts show Iran was unable to achieve the self-supply of textile products at that time, notwithstanding a certain

[5]It was enacted on 6th of Esfand in 1309 (February 25, 1931) and another law, the Enlarged Edition of the Law of Government's Monopoly in Foreign Trade (qānūn-e motammem-e qānūn-e enhesār-e tejārat-e khārejī)with more comprehensive contents was enacted on 20th of the same month. (Rūz-nāme-ye rasmī-ye Jomhūrī-ye Eslāmī-ye Īrān 2009, 476–478).

increase in domestic production under the government's industrialization strategy. Under the government-imposed trade monopoly, in any case, it was clearly expected that local textile enterprises would play a major role in modern industrialization alongside state-owned enterprises.

2.1.2 *Post-World War II Period*

The occupation by the Allied forces seriously damaged Iran's economy during the war. Consequently, the industrialization process started before the war was physically interrupted. Therefore, the first emergent task for postwar Iran became rehabilitation of the national economy, with a focus on postwar reconstruction. At the same time, Mohammad Reza Shah (1941–79 on the throne), who ascended after Reza Shah, also faced an immediate need to settle the domestic political disorder caused by a series of ethnic separatist movements after the war.

The Iranian government followed the old import-substitution strategy for some time after the war. The government bolstered up the textile, sugar-refining, and steel industries in order to stimulate relatively weak private manufacturing investment. The state-owned factories established in Reza Shah's era were again opened. The introduction of a preferential tax and material import system for industrial production also served to promote private investment.

A more aggressive economic development strategy was discussed in this period, including reorganizing existing state-owned enterprises and formulation of a development plan. In 1946, some government officials emphasized the necessity of having such a development plan, pointing out that a laissez-faire policy was not suitable for Iran, which had never experienced economic development. Plan Organization (Sāzmān-e Bar-nāme), the nucleus of the new development plans, was set up in 1949. An American consultancy (Overseas Consultants Incorporated) took responsibility for the specific planning, a step Iran took because the World Bank requested Iran to submit a detailed development plan when the Iranian government asked them for financial aid.[6] Iran's industrialization strategy, however, greatly transformed after this planning as a result of oil nationalization in 1951.

In March 1951, the parliament approved the oil nationalization bill and thus ended the Iranian oil concessions that had been held by Britain (via the Anglo-Iranian Oil Company) since the beginning of the twentieth century. In the subsequent 2 years of Mosaddeq's premiership, who took over the leadership of

---

[6]Along with the start of the World Bank Group, including International Bank of Reconstruction and Development (IBRD), development funds began to be disbursed to developing countries as well as postwar rehabilitation funds allocated to advanced countries. It is thought that these efforts noticeably reflected the argument for postwar economic recovery in those days, mainly in the US, which aimed at to achieve complete employment, prevent protective trade, secure stable economic growth and such, for the sake of realization of "reconstruction of the free trade system."

Iran's oil nationalization movement, public favor toward nationalism and democratization continued to shake the Shah's political foundation.

Given ongoing political disturbances due to the oil nationalization movement, the investment environment for domestic manufacturing was not very stable. The country remained entrenched in postwar reconstruction. In the public sector, the budget for the mining and manufacturing industries suffered drastic cuts in the middle of first National Development Plan (1949–55) owing to the oil nationalization movement. In private sector, too, an unstable situation continued. New factories were established in order to respond the demand growth for domestic products caused by a foreign currency shortage. But when the foreign currency situation improved and prices of imported goods dropped, these producers immediately suffered from surplus stock.

When the oil nationalization movement came to a standstill after a coup in 1953, the Shah gained another supporter: the US, who replaced Britain and increased its presence in Iran. A new political situation appeared. Rapid increases of oil income as a result of oil nationalization and the sequent political stabilization secured the expansion of manufacturing production and investment. The government advocated the same "import substituting industrialization" as in Reza Shah's era to protect and develop the private sector. Ample funds were supplied to the private sector through various industrial banks, backed by sufficient oil income (Benedick 1964).

During and after the third National Development Plan (1962–68), the government's investment priority shifted to heavy industries from light industries. But importing commodities was prohibited when similar goods were produced in Iran, and many privileges such as tax holiday were given to domestic enterprises. Overall manufacturing production grew by 12.9% per annum in 1963–72 (United Nations 1975, 231).

Textile industry, which was one of the priority industries just after the war, gradually faded from the center of the government's industrialization strategy. The macro trend of Iran's textile production at that time was as follows.

Textile production grew 11.5% on average per annum during the 9 years in 1963–72 (United Nations 1975, 231). Its ratio to the whole manufacturing production, however, dropped rapidly from 28.9% in 1959 to 16.6% in 1972. Investment in textiles also expanded in parallel with production but its ratio to the whole manufacturing investment dropped from 23% in 1962 to 10.9% in 1972 (Ministry of Industry and Mines 1976, 10–11).

The import–export trend of the period indicates that Iran's fabric imports were quite limited due to the import control policy until 1972, it is thought that Iran was importing yarn and producing fabric domestically until that time. As for cotton fabric, the fact that barely any cotton yarn was imported while raw cotton was exported suggests that cotton yarn was almost self-supplied (Iwasaki 1993, 69).

Demand growth accompanying the improving national standard of living had been already witnessed since the beginning of the 1960s. It is plausible that Iran's textile industry responded to this trend until at least 1972 by expanding the production although the some raw materials depended on imports.

Under these circumstances, the state of firms and workers in the textile industry changed as given below. Many new manufacturing firms were established in the

1960s. Concerning the number of textile firms, only fragmentary data are available from the end of 1950s until the mid-1980s. The number of firms with more than 10 workers (hereafter called large-scale firms)[7] increased by 150% in a decade from 863 in 1962 to 1367 in 1972 (Ministry of Interior 1964, 10); (Ministry of Industry and Mines 1976, 36).[8] It seems plausible that a large number of new textile firms were established between the end of 1950s and the beginning of 1960s in general (Iwasaki 1993, 69–70). On the other hand, the actual number of firms with fewer than 10 workers (hereafter called small-scale firms) through this period is not known. According to the 1962 Industrial Census, the number of small-scale firms was reported to be 6170, amounting to 87% of the whole (Ministry of Interior 1964, 10).

How has the number of workers employed by firms changed? According to the breakdown by industry type, out of all workers employed by large manufacturing firms in 1947, approximately 60% worked in the textile industry (Bharier 1971, 179). The textile industry contributed considerably to employment supply in manufacturing, although the state of small-scale firms was unknown. The data from Ministry of Industry and Mines also indicate that the number of workers in the textile and carpet (as well as apparel) industries increased continuously between 1962 and 1972 (see Table 2.1). It reached nearly 160 thousand in 1972, and its ratio to all manufacturing workers maintained about 25%. Incidentally, the number of workers in apparel industry at that point of time was about 93 thousand (Ministry of Industry and Mines 1976, 6). It is remarkable that the contribution of the textile and apparel industry to the employment supply was outstanding compared to that of other industries.

Although public investment increasingly prioritized modern sectors and shifted away from traditional sectors like textiles after the oil nationalization, the protective trade policy operating under the industrialization strategy since 1930s helped the textile industry survive. Iran's textile industry, which employed the most workers in the manufacturing sector and where private firms were the pillar of the industry, barely continued to respond to domestic demand, instead partially relying on imported raw materials.

Nevertheless, Iran's textile imports grew rapidly after 1972, possibly due to drastic changes in the domestic economic environment concerning the textile (and apparel) industry. The government's oil income jumped to approximately fivefold owing to the steep rise in oil prices in 1973. Import restrictions on scarce textile products were greatly relaxed. The old import-substitution industrialization strategy, which had been previously advocated, was in fact abandoned.

---

[7]This denomination is based on the division in Iran's official statistics. The data on manufacturing firms including textile and apparel that Statistical Centre of Iran (Markaz-e Āmār-e Īrān) provide are classified by the number of workers. Firm with more than 10 workers are customarily categorized as "large-scale firms" (kār-gāh-hā-ye san'atī-ye bozorg).

[8]The number of large-scale apparel-producing firms was reported as 365 in the 1972 data (Ministry of Industry and Mines 1976, 36).

Table 2.1 The number of workers employed in textile and carpet industry 1962–72

	Textile and carpet (a)	Whole manufacturing (b)	a/b (%)
1962	69,272	249,589	27.8
1963	82,428	290,432	28.4
1964	107,494	338,469	31.8
1965	124,687	372,474	33.5
1966	127,216	388,850	32.7
1967	131,437	461,488	28.5
1968	142,401	462,215	30.8
1969	148,209	530,462	27.9
1970	151,454	547,343	27.7
1971	157,554	581,250	27.1
1972	159,243	616,254	25.8

Source Ministry of Industry and Mines (1976)

Figure 2.1 shows that after this period, more troubles emerged in the self-supply of domestic cotton products. Fluctuations in the exchange rate after the oil crisis, the subsequent decline of Iran's export competitiveness, and shrinking of the carpet market due to recession experienced by its trade partners led Iran's exports to a fall after 1975. That is to say, de facto "import liberalization" began to exert a negative influence on the textile industry after the oil crisis, although domestic production continued to expand.

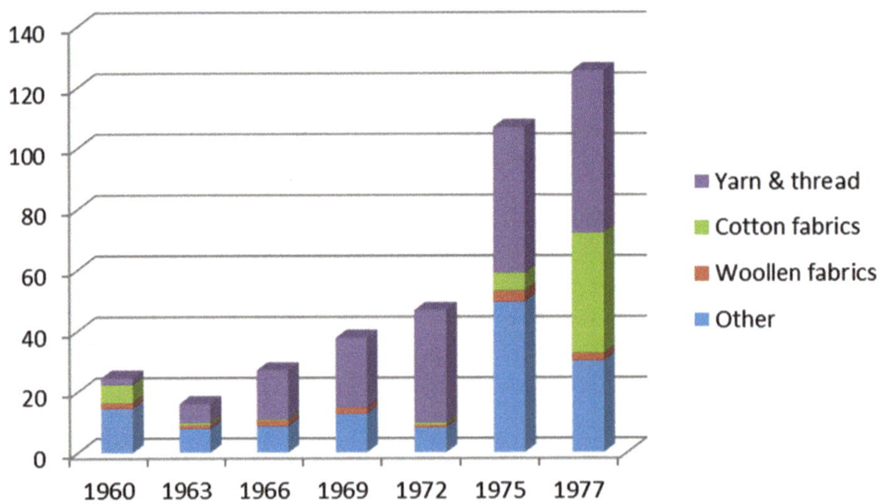

Fig. 2.1 Change in volume of textile import (1960–77). *Note* A unit of weight: thousand metric ton. *Source* United Nations, Yearbook of International Trade Statistics (1965, 1967, 1969, 1974, 1978, 1982)

2.1.3 *Textile and Apparel Industry After the 1979 Revolution*

This import liberalization trend, however, was again disturbed for 10-odd years by the Revolution in 1979. Impatient "Westernization" policies forged by the Shah and his alliance with the US aroused criticism throughout the country, and consequently, the Pahlavi regime fell when Islamic jurists grabbed political power.

Iran then faced serious international isolation after they declared a new form of government known as "Islamic Republicanism." Following the revolution, Iran broke off relations with the US, which had previously backed the country. A heavy decline in the exchange rate, coupled with economic sanctions, impeded Iran's ability to trade freely with foreign countries. The Iran–Iraq War broke out, following Iraq's invasion, and continued for 8 years, causing oil income to fall. The government was compelled to put the country on a severely controlled economic system. A prohibition on introducing foreign capital and import restrictions on Western consumer goods were, indeed, not only to boost the government's financial position but also to reflect its cultural policy, which intended to prevent the inflow of unpleasant Western culture at the beginning of the revolutionary era. As a consequence, Iran's manufacturing industries were once again put under protective policies and given a means of survival so that they could respond to domestic demand. It goes without saying that the textile and apparel industry was not exempted.

On the other hand, Iran's predisposition to relying on imported intermediate and capital goods, which originated in the Pahlavi era, was never eliminated. The government supported domestic firms by intervening in the currency market and fixing the exchange rate, thus allowing the gap between the market rate and the fixed rate to be filled by the oil income in order to maintain manufacturing production. Considerable subsidies were disbursed to manufacturing firms, which were requisitioned and nationalized after the revolution.

In this period, the government set up Centers for Procurement and Distribution (marākez-e tahīye va touzī'-e kālā) for direct control of imports. The centers were solely responsible for importing the necessary goods as classified by industry and item, and then supplied domestic firms. The system originated in the wartime economic policy that had mainly focused on exchange rate control and commodities allocation during the Iran–Iraq War (1980–1988), and the restrictions continued in the same way after the ceasefire. Imports of intermediate goods such as raw materials and machinery for domestic manufacturing became totally under the government's control, with only some institutions, firms, and individuals being granted import permission to secure access. In this system, the centers themselves purchased goods from suppliers abroad. The majority of the goods were distributed to domestic state-owned firms through the centers. In parallel with this system, firms and factories with special permission from the government could purchase foreign goods directly. Although private firms were to be treated as possible purchasers in the system, the actual buyers were mainly the big state-owned companies. Private firms without an "import license," equivalent to foreign currency allocation, were obliged to buy imported goods from the centers or the end suppliers in the domestic market.

These postrevolution economic policies, which combined wartime economic necessities and protectionism, caused severe negative economic effects, such as inefficiency, weak financial standing, and rent-seeking. Consequently, revision of these policies and "liberalization" began to be discussed early in the 1990s. President Khātamī (1997–2005 in office)'s government greatly promoted liberalization, which was symbolized by privatization of state-owned firms, a move that accelerated the considerable change in trade policy. Meanwhile, restrictions on foreign currency were temporarily eased due to the rapid increase of oil income while the domestic market expanded greatly due to postwar population growth.

As far as the textile and apparel industry is concerned, the influence of this change in trade policies came to be felt only after 2000. This delay in impact reflects the fact that the import–export business continued to be controlled by a license system, although the above-mentioned procurement centers gradually lost their leverage and almost ceased to function by the end of the 1990s.

Trends from the beginning of 1970s through to today can be understood to some degree by following the data from the Statistical Centre of Iran (Markaz-e Āmār-e Īrān, hereafter MAI). Iran's textile and apparel industry was also exposed to such changes in business environment caused by substantial political upheavals.

The MAI figures mainly concern large-scale firms, with exceptions in some years. Their figures reveal that the output (in real terms) of Iran's textile industry remained mostly steady in the three decades between 1350 (in the Gregorian calendar 1971/72) and 1390 (2011/12), peaking around 1992. The number of workers in large-scale firms remained around 140–150 thousand throughout the 1980s and 1990s, and continued to be one of the biggest sources of employment. The total number of workers, including those working in small-scale firms, is available for some years from 1987. These figures show that total number of workers in the textile industry exceeded 430 thousand, which corresponds to 30% of all manufacturing workers. Production in this period increased, possibly due to the expanded wartime demand and import restrictions.

What deserves special mention is that a certain level of production was upheld despite the upheavals of revolution and war. This could possibly reflect the fact that large factories were nationalized and put under the protection of the revolutionary government, while the rapid expansion of domestic demand can be attributed to population growth, which constantly encouraged the entry of private funds.[9] It is not plausible, however, to conclude that domestic production sufficiently responded to the demand. The steady imports perhaps made up for shortages in textile products like yarn and fabrics.

The number of workers in large-scale textile firms began to decrease swiftly after 2000, and fell below 80 thousand in 2011, a change largely attributable to

[9]Population of Iran is reported as approximately 33 million in 1355 (1976/77), and 75 million in 1390 (2011/12), respectively (Markaz-e Āmār-e Īrān 2014, 98).

termination of preferential treatment toward state-owned firms under the "liberalization" policies. The share to the whole manufacturing dropped to 6%, while food processing and motorcycle production came to occupy superior positions in the employment supply (Markaz-e Āmār-e Īrān 2014, 338).

The apparel industry used to be included in general textile industry. As mentioned earlier, the trend of the textile industry as a whole after the Second World War can be inferred from the statistical data to some extent. But it is not chronologically clear the extent to which textile production comprised apparel production, while woven fabrics were traditionally the main product of Iran's textile industry.

Up through 1372 (1993/94), the statistical data categorized textile, apparel, and leather industries as the same industry, and no breakdown into these subcategories was given in most cases. In the middle of 1990s, homemade apparel and small made-to-order tailors (shakhsī-dūz) were still rather common; therefore, it is supposed that Iran's ready-made apparel industry does not have a very long history (Iwasaki 2000, 97).

Nonetheless, it seems apparent that the apparel industry, as well as textile industry, relied heavily upon imported machinery and raw materials. As the next chapter will explore in detail, fieldworks conducted by the author since 1990s have shown that both relatively large-scale and small-scale firms used imported goods for production. Accordingly, the business environment surrounding the apparel industry may not have been very different from that of the textile industry. There are, however, some exceptional data in some years that offer insight into movements that occurred in the apparel industry. For example, the number of workers in the apparel industry in 1972 was reported to be about 93 thousand, as mentioned earlier. During 1359 (1980/81) and 1364 (1985/86), there were some 200 large-scale apparel firms in the country[10] and approximately 5 thousand people were employed (Markaz-e Āmār-e Īrān 1983, 1984, 1985, 1986, 1987, 1988). The production level of these firms comprised 0.6% of the whole manufacturing production.

2.2 Iran's Apparel Industry According to Recent Statistical Data

2.2.1 Scale of the Apparel Industry

A category of "apparel industry" was created under the overarching category of "textile industry" in Iran's statistical data in 1373 (1994/95). Apparel products thus came to be distinguished clearly from other textile products. The data for 1373

[10]The number of large-scale apparel-producing firms in the country was reported 632 in 1360 (1981/82) but it is rather an unreliable figure in the light of figures of year before and after (Markaz-e Āmār-e Īrān 1985).

(1994/95), 1375 (1996/97), and 1381 (2002/03) include figures for small-scale firms; therefore, it is possible to conjecture trends for the whole apparel industry.

The number of workers in the apparel industry in 1373(1994/95) was reported to be about 98 thousand, which was almost the same level as in 1972 (Markaz-e Āmār-e Īrān 1998, 207). Although this number decreased to 87 thousand at one point (Markaz-e Āmār-e Īrān 1999, 250), it rose to 126 thousand again in 1381 (2002/03) (Markaz-e Āmār-e Īrān 2004, 265). A total of 45 thousand firms operated in the sector in 1373 (1994/95) (Markaz-e Āmār-e Īrān 1998, 200), falling to 38 thousand in 1375 (1996/97) (Markaz-e Āmār-e Īrān 1999, 243), and rising to 58 thousand in 1381 (2002/03) (Markaz-e Āmār-e Īrān 2004, 258), respectively.

The salient point here is that a quite large proportion of firms were small-scale, and accordingly, a large proportion of workers worked for small-scale firms. Out of all workers in apparel industry, those working in small-scale firms accounted for 87% in 1373, 88% in 1375, and 93% in 1381, respectively. The proportion of small-scale firms also amounted to 98% in 1373, 98% in 1375, and 99% in 1381. Thus, the industry was predominantly composed of small-scale firms with fewer than 10 workers each.[11]

This is an important point when we consider the main drivers of Iran's apparel production. The output data show that those small-scale firms produced most of the value added generated by the entire apparel industry, that is 74.8% in 1373, 79.3% in 1375, and 84.9% in 1381 (Markaz-e Āmār-e Īrān 1998, 216, 1999, 263, 2004, 273). These facts indicate that those small-scale firms can be considered the most important pillar in Iran's apparel production.

It is not possible to grasp today's status accurately since the relevant statistical data concerning the small-scale firms with fewer than 10 workers have been not published for years after 1381 (2002/03). In any case, further discussion starting from an assumption that the minuteness of firms is the special characteristics of Iran's apparel industry will be appropriate.

Following data from other years that concerned only large-scale firms is not sufficiently precise to catch the real trends of Iran's apparel industry, as a substantial portion of its production comes from small-scale firms.[12] Taking this characteristic into account, we can now examine the trends of large-scale firms. The total number of firms decreased by one-third in the period 1376 (1997/98)–1390 (2011/12) (see Table 2.2). The state-owned firms, originally few in number, almost disappeared. The number of middle-scale firms with 10–49 workers, however, fluctuated widely and therefore cannot be considered to have shown a constant trend toward decline. The number of workers peaked at 12 thousand in 1373 (1994/95) (Markaz-e Āmār-e Īrān 1998, 207), and then decreased rapidly to 5 thousand in 1379 (2000/01) (Markaz-e Āmār-e Īrān 2002, 256) (see Table 2.3). As the number of

[11]The ratio of number of apparel-producing firms to all manufacturing firms was 12% in 1373 (1994/95) (Markaz-e Āmār-e Īrān 1998, 200), rising to 13% in 1381 (2002/03) (Markaz-e Āmār-e Īrān 2004, 259).

[12]For textile production excluding apparel, the trend can be grasped to a certain degree based on MAI data since in the fields of spinning or reeling, large-scale firms are the main actors.

Table 2.2 Change in number of apparel-producing firms by classified by number of workers 1998–2012

	1–9 workers	10–49 workers	50–99 workers	More than 100 workers
1376(1997/98)		376(1)	8(5)	10(9)
1377(1998/99)		380(2)	8(5)	6(5)
1378 (1999/2000)		127(1)	9(1)	7(2)
1379(2000/01)		109(2)	11(2)	7(1)
1380(2001/02)		119(2)	11(3)	8(1)
1381(2002/03)	58,538(0)	339(2)	18(1)	9(1)
1382(2003/04)		263(0)	21(0)	10(1)
1383(2004/05)		206(3)	15(0)	9(0)
1384(2005/06)		182(1)	13(0)	11(0)
1385(2006/07)		151(0)	10(1)	12(0)
1386(2007/08)		135(1)	16(1)	14(0)
1387(2008/09)		N.D	N.D	N.D
1388(2009/10)		133(1)	17(0)	17(0)
1389(2010/11)		116(0)	9(0)	22(0)
1390(2011/12)		103(1)	12(0)	16(0)

Note The figures in round brackets are the number of state-owned firms. *Source* Markaz-e Āmār-e Īrān (2000/01, 2001, 2002, 2003, 2004, 2005, 2006/07, 2007/08, 2008/09, 2011, 2012, 2013, 2014)

firms and workers in the entire apparel industry rose in this period, as mentioned earlier, it can be assumed that firm scale within the industry shrank in the latter half of the 1990s.

2.2.2 *Apparel Production and Import Liberalization*

Output (in real terms) from large-scale apparel firms remained on almost the same level in 1376 (1997/98)–1388 (2009/10) and increased after the end of 2000s, with an exceptional period occurring from the late 1990s until 2000, when output suddenly decreased by half (Markaz-e Āmār-e Īrān 1999, 2000/01, 2002, 2003, 2004, 2005, 2006/07, 2007/08, 2008/09, 2011, 2012, 2013, 2014). It can be observed that large-scale firms barely maintained a stable output level even as the number of firms and workers greatly decreased.

On the other hand, the proportion of apparel output (including that from small-scale firms) out of all manufacturing output dropped to about 1.4% in 1381 from 2.3% in 1373 (Markaz-e Āmār-e Īrān 2004,273). The trend after this date is unknown at the moment.

Table 2.3 Change in number of workers in apparel-producing firms classified by number of workers 1995–2012

	1–9 workers	More than 10 workers
1373(1994/95)	85,862	12,734
1374(1995/96)		N.D
1375(1996/97)	77,287	10,209
1376(1997/98)		9066
1377(1998/99)		7546
1378(1999/2000)		5112
1379(2000/01)		5049
1380(2001/02)		5151
1381(2002/03)	117,955	8859
1382(2003/04)		8585
1383(2004/05)		7188
1384(2005/06)		6605
1385(2006/07)		6504
1386(2007/08)		7003
1387(2008/09)		N.D
1388(2009/10)		7973
1389(2010/11)		7856
1390(2011/12)		7366

Source Markaz-e Āmār-e Īrān (1998, 1999, 2000/01, 2001, 2002, 2003, 2004, 2005, 2006/07, 2007/08, 2008/09, 2011, 2012, 2013, 2014)

As already mentioned, the period between the end of 1990s and the beginning of 2000s saw the government's "liberalization" policies begin to influence the textile and apparel industries. The conventional control system regarding the import of raw materials was eased, and the goods that the domestic distributors brought in appeared on the market. In this sense, the business environment improved for apparel firms, who needed to procure foreign fabrics and accessories. Possibly due to the relatively better commodity supply and a domestic market exhibiting lively demand, the number of small-scale apparel firms swelled in this period.[13]

[13]Prior to liberalization, the Iran's import controls were enforced by an assortment of policies: foreign exchange allocation, introduction of "import permission items" by the Ministries of Commerce, Industry and Mines, and imposition of high duties (basic tariff plus commercial profit tax). Although the trade policy change was never explicitly announced, conditions relating to apparel imports were removed after 1380 (2001/02). At the same time, the tariff rate was reduced considerably from 200 to 90%. This was again reduced to 50% in 1383 (2004/05), but raised to 100% in 1385 (2006/07), where it has remained ever since (Directorate-General for Export-Import Regulations 2004, 2005, 2006; Edāre-ye Koll-e Moqarrarāt-e Sāderāt o Vāredāt-e Vezārat-e Bāzargānī 2000, 2003, 2004, 2005; Trade Promotion Organization of Iran, Directorate-General for Export-Import Regulations 2008; Sāzmān-e Touse'e-ye Tejārat-e Īrān, Edāre-ye Koll-e Moqarrarāt-e Sāderāt o Vāredāt 2011).

Nevertheless, although apparel products were hard to find in the domestic market because of severe import controls on final consumer goods import restrictions on these products were also substantially relaxed. The following chapters will fully examine influence of these relaxations on Iran's apparel production as a whole. The actual statistical data concerning the apparel trade are provided below. Iranian export of apparel products (in terms of volume) expanded constantly up to about 1382 (2003/04) and then gradually decreased until 1389 (2010/11), when it fell considerably (see Table 2.4). This exactly coincided with the tightening of economic sanctions toward Iran by Western countries. Furthermore, the output of large-scale apparel firms, who were the main exporters, remained level. Therefore, the drop in export was more attributable to restrictions in foreign trade other than to the domestic production environment.

Meanwhile, apparel imports surged in the same period (see Table 2.4). Iran's apparel imports were almost negligible in 1990s. But the data indicate that they swelled rapidly after 1382 (2003/04). The volume of imported apparel products in 1382 was approximately 11 times as much as that in 1381 (see Fig. 2.2). As mentioned previously, a huge quantity of foreign apparel goods (especially Chinese) poured into Iran in this period. The trade data figures substantiate this occurrence.

The import volume declined markedly in 1385 (2006/07), but increased again in 1387 (2008/09). Taken together, these findings indicate that compared to previous times, an enormous quantity of foreign apparel goods began to flow steadily into Iran after 1382.

Table 2.4 Change in volume of apparel export and import 1999–2013

	Export (ton)	Import (ton)
1377(1998/99)	3406	29
1378(1999/2000)	6307	1
1379(2000/01)	10,005	6
1380(2001/02)	12,896	14
1381(2002/03)	14,064	145
1382(2003/04)	16,815	1597
1383(2004/05)	12,033	5640
1384(2005/06)	12,592	6182
1385(2006/07)	10,825	975
1386(2007/08)	10,038	1270
1387(2008/09)	8589	1973
1388(2009/10)	11,581	2055
1389(2010/11)	6594	2432
1390(2011/12)	5054	2212
1391(2012/13)	5131	1771

Source Markaz-e Āmār-e Īrān (2000/01, 2001, 2002, 2003, 2004, 2005, 2006/07, 2007/08, 2008/09, 2011, 2012, 2013, 2014)

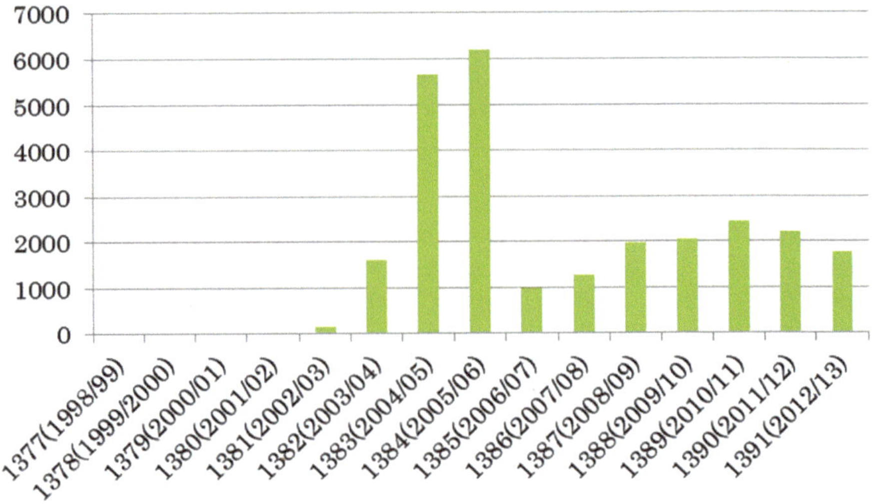

Fig. 2.2 Change in volume of apparel import (1999–2013). *Note* A unit of weight:ton. *Source* Markaz-e Āmār-e Īrān (2000/01–2014)

As stated above, the production and business environment for Iran's apparel industry, and for its parent, the textile industry, was never quite stable. In particular, the fact that the government's industrialization strategy was de facto abandoned owing to the rapid growth of oil income seriously hindered the textile industry's development, although it had been ranked as the national mainstay industry from the modernization era until oil nationalization as part of the strategy to realize import substitution. Moreover, restrictions on textile and apparel products were repeatedly imposed and relaxed according to changes in terms of trade caused by political circumstances. The fact that the apparel industry was given a role as a control valve for the country's balance of payments can be said to have exerted a great negative influence on the business management strategy of apparel firms, regardless of their scale. Meanwhile, strong demand backed by one of the biggest markets in the Middle East continuously attracted private investment.

Consequently, the industry was never absolutely destroyed despite repeated rises and falls, and thus was able to maintain a certain presence among Iran's manufacturing industries. It is rather noticeable that Iran's apparel industry has managed to supply products to the domestic market so far despite its minuteness in firm scale under the above-mentioned unstable business environment.

It is therefore necessary for an analysis of the performance of Iran's apparel industry to focus not only on the macro conditions and environment but also on the organizations within the industry, as mentioned at the beginning of this book. The following chapters will discuss the characteristics of Iran's apparel firms and their organization based on the author's fieldwork conducted in Tehran, the country's biggest apparel-producing center, mainly from the perspective of firms' tolerance of quite an unstable business environment.

References

Benedick, R. E. (1964). *Industrial finance in Iran: A study of financial practice in an underdeveloped economy*. Boston: Harvard University.
Bharier, J. (1971). *Economic development in Iran 1900–1970*. London: Oxford University Press.
Directorate-General for Export-Import Regulations. (2004). *Export-Import Regulation Act 2004–2005*. Tehran.
Directorate-General for Export-Import Regulations. (2005). *Export-Import Regulation Act 2005–2006*. Tehran.
Directorate-General for Export-Import Regulations. (2006). *Export-Import Regulation Act 2006–2007*. Tehran.
Edāre-ye Koll-e Moqarrarāt-e Sāderāt o Vāredāt-e Vezārat-e Bāzargānī. (2000). *Moqarrarāt-e Sāderāt o Vāredāt va Jadāvel-e Zamīme-ye Ān, 1379 (Export-Import Regulations)*. Tehrān.
Edāre-ye Koll-e Moqarrarāt-e Sāderāt o Vāredāt-e Vezārat-e Bāzargānī (2003) *Moqarrarāt-e Sāderāt o Vāredāt va Jadāvel-e Zamīme-ye Ān, Sāl-e 1382 (Export-Import Regulations)*. Tehrān.
Edāre-ye Koll-e Moqarrarāt-e Sāderāt o Vāredāt-e Vezārat-e Bāzargānī. (2004). *Moqarrarāt-e Sāderāt o Vāredāt va Jadāvel-e Zamīme-ye Ān, Sāl-e 1383 (Export-Import Regulations)*. Tehrān.
Edāre-ye Koll-e Moqarrarāt-e Sāderāt o Vāredāt-e Vezārat-e Bāzargānī. (2005). *Moqarrarāt-e Sāderāt o Vāredāt va Jadāvel-e Zamīme-ye Ān, Sāl-e 1384 (Export-Import Regulations)*. Tehrān.
Gotō, A. (2000). Iran ni okeru Kokumin keizai no Keisei: Taisen-kanki no Mondai (Iranian Economy between Two World Wars). *Iran Kokumin Keizai no Dainamizumu (The Dynamism of Iranian National Economy)* (pp. 3–39). Chiba: Institute of Developing Economies.
Issawi, Ch. (Ed.). (1971). *The economic history of Iran 1800–1914*. Chicago: The University of Chicago Press.
Issawi, Ch. (1982). *An economic history of the Middle East and North Africa*. London: Methuen.
Iwasaki, Y. (1993). Iran Sen'i Sangyō Gaikan: Jūkyū Seiki shotō kara Isuramu Kakumei made no Rekishiteki Hatten. (A Historical Survey on the in Iran). *Gendai no Chūtō (The Contemporary Middle East), 15,* 61–75.
Iwasaki, Y. (2000). Iran no Seisan Soshiki to Ryūtsū kikō: Teheran Apareru Sangyō no Jirei. (The System of Production and Distribution in Iran: A Case Study of the Apparel Industry in Tehran). *Iran Kokumin Keizai no Dainamizumu. (The Dynamism of Iranian National Economy)* (pp. 93–129). Chiba: Institute of Developing Economies.
Markaz-e Āmār-e Īrān. (1983). *Sāl-nāme-ye Āmārī 1360 (Iran Statistical Yearbook)*, Tehrān.
Markaz-e Āmār-e Īrān. (1984). *Sāl-nāme-ye Āmārī 1361 (Iran Statistical Yearbook)*, Tehrān.
Markaz-e Āmār-e Īrān. (1985). *Sāl-nāme-ye Āmārī 1362 (Iran Statistical Yearbook)*, Tehrān.
Markaz-e Āmār-e Īrān. (1986). *Sāl-nāme-ye Āmārī 1363 (Iran Statistical Yearbook)*, Tehrān.
Markaz-e Āmār-e Īrān. (1987). *Sāl-nāme-ye Āmārī 1364 (Iran Statistical Yearbook)*, Tehrān.
Markaz-e Āmār-e Īrān. (1988). *Sāl-nāme-ye Āmārī 1365 (Iran Statistical Yearbook)*, Tehrān.
Markaz-e Āmār-e Īrān. (1998). *Sāl-nāme-ye Āmārī-ye Keshvar 1375 (Iran Statistical Yearbook)*, Tehrān.
Markaz-e Āmār-e Īrān. (1999). *Sāl-nāme-ye Āmārī-ye Keshvar 1376 (Iran Statistical Yearbook)*, Tehrān.
Markaz-e Āmār-e Īrān. (2000/01). *Sāl-nāme-ye Āmārī-ye Keshvar 1378 (Iran Statistical Yearbook)*, Tehrān.
Markaz-e Āmār-e Īrān. (2001). *Sāl-nāme-ye Āmārī-ye Keshvar 1379 (Iran Statistical Yearbook)*, Tehrān.
Markaz-e Āmār-e Īrān. (2002). *Sāl-nāme-ye Āmārī-ye Keshvar 1380 (Iran Statistical Yearbook)*, Tehrān.
Markaz-e Āmār-e Īrān. (2003). *Sāl-nāme-ye Āmārī-ye Keshvar 1381 (Iran Statistical Yearbook)*, Tehrān.

Markaz-e Āmār-e Īrān. (2004). *Sāl-nāme-ye Āmārī-ye Keshvar 1382 (Iran Statistical Yearbook)*, Tehrān.

Markaz-e Āmār-e Īrān. (2005). *Sāl-nāme-ye Āmārī-ye Keshvar 1383 (Iran Statistical Yearbook)*, Tehrān.

Markaz-e Āmār-e Īrān. (2006/07). *Sāl-nāme-ye Āmārī-ye Keshvar 1384 (Iran Statistical Yearbook)*, Tehrān.

Markaz-e Āmār-e Īrān. (2007/08). *Sāl-nāme-ye Āmārī-ye Keshvar 1385 (Iran Statistical Yearbook)*, Tehrān.

Markaz-e Āmār-e Īrān. (2008/09). *Sāl-nāme-ye Āmārī-ye Keshvar 1386 (Iran Statistical Yearbook)*, Tehrān.

Markaz-e Āmār-e Īrān. (2011). *Sāl-nāme-ye Āmārī-ye Keshvar 1388 (Iran Statistical Yearbook)*, Tehrān.

Markaz-e Āmār-e Īrān. (2012). *Sāl-nāme-ye Āmārī-ye Keshvar 1389 (Iran Statistical Yearbook)*, Tehrān.

Markaz-e Āmār-e Īrān. (2013). *Sāl-nāme-ye Āmārī-ye Keshvar 1390 (Iran Statistical Yearbook)*, Tehrān.

Markaz-e Āmār-e Īrān. (2014). *Sāl-nāme-ye Āmārī-ye Keshvar 1391 (Iran Statistical Yearbook)*, Tehrān.

Ministry of Industry and Mines. (1976). *Iranian Industrial Statistics 1972*. Tehran.

Ministry of Interior. (1964). *Industrial census of Iran 1963: Manufacture of textile in Urban Areas*. Tehran: The Plan Organization.

Rabizadeh, M. M. (1975). (Trans. from Russian by Kato, K.). *Nijisseiki Sanjū Nendai no Iran Kōgyō ni okeru Shihonshugiteki Kigyō no Hatten. (The development of capitalistic enterprises of Iran in 1930s)*. Tokyo: Institute of Developing Economies.

Rūz-nāme-ye Rasmī-ye Jomhūrī-ye Eslāmī-ye Īrān. (2009). *Majmū'e-ye Qavānīn va Moqarrarāt-e Sāl-hā-ye 1300–1312 Bakhsh-e Avval (Collections of Laws and Regulations)*. Tehrān.

Sāzmān-e Touse'e-ye Tejārat-e Īrān, Edāre-ye Koll-e Moqarrarāt-e Sāderāt o Vāredāt. (2011). *Moqarrarāt-e Sāderāt o Vāredāt-e Sāl-e 90 (Export-Import Regualtions)*. Tehrān.

Trade Promotion Organization of Iran, Directorate-General for Export-Import Regulations. (2008). *Export-Import Regulation Act 2008–2009*. Tehran.

United Nations. (1953). *Yearbook of International Trade Statistics 1952*. New York: The Statistical Office of the United Nations.

United Nations. (1965). *Yearbook of International Trade Statistics 1963*. New York: The Statistical Office of the United Nations.

United Nations. (1967). *Yearbook of International Trade Statistics 1965*. New York: The Statistical Office of the United Nations.

United Nations. (1969). *Yearbook of International Trade Statistics 1967*. New York: The Statistical Office of the United Nations.

United Nations. (1974). *Yearbook of International Trade Statistics 1972–73*. New York: The Statistical Office of the United Nations.

United Nations. (1975). *The Growth of World Industry 1973 Edition* (Vol. I). New York: The Statistical Office of the United Nations.

United Nations. (1978). *Yearbook of International Trade Statistics 1977*. New York: The Statistical Office of the United Nations.

United Nations. (1982). *Yearbook of International Trade Statistics 1981*. New York: The Statistical Office of the United Nations.

Chapter 3
Characteristics of Apparel-Producing Organization

Abstract Tehran is home to the foremost apparel-producing center in Iran, where the author conducted fieldwork in the 1990s and 2000s. This primary research enabled the clarification of the following points: larger firms relied less on outsourcing, product planning was carried out by the firms themselves, and few firms had direct relations with retailers. They also tended to avoid establishing strong ties with outside contractors in production, although outsourcing has become more common. The overwhelming majority of apparel-producing firms is very small in scale, but they are generally not involved in vertical integration with large-scale firms. In addition, although they often put out works to other small-scale firms, a joint-stock partnership is never observed. As for large-scale firms, the relationships between firms and contractors are temporary and flexible too. As a result of the absence of industrial consolidation, large-scale firms remain relatively small compared with highly integrated firms abroad. On the whole, the diminutiveness and independence of these firms can be pointed out as extremely prominent features of industrial organization in Iran's apparel-producing industry.

Keywords Apparel-producing center · Patterns of apparel-producing firms in Iran · Fieldwork in Tehran · Questionnaire survey on apparel firms

3.1 Tehran: The Biggest Producing Center

This chapter will provide a general overview of the organizational characteristics of Iranian apparel firms. Before beginning the discussion of the typical pattern of Iranian apparel-producing firms, some background on the apparel-producing center in Tehran where the author conducted fieldwork should be given. This will be useful because the aforesaid statistical data from which some characteristics of Iran's apparel industry on the whole were inferred shows little about the local features of each district.

In many other countries (and areas), certain places or districts are often known as textile and apparel goods producing centers, as a number of firms are gather and

Y. Iwasaki, *Industrial Organization in Iran*, SpringerBriefs in Economics,
DOI 10.1007/978-981-10-4579-0_3

operate side by side in these locations. It is frequently pointed out that such an agglomeration emerges since economies of scale can be achieved in various aspects such as procurement of raw materials, information sharing, transportation, and division of production process. The same phenomenon is also observed in Iran.

The statistical data about the geographical concentration of apparel firms are only fragmentary as the number of firms classified by province (*ostān*) and industry are not always published. In view of the following points, however, it is quite evident that Tehran is home to the biggest apparel-producing center in Iran.

According to the directory published by MAI, large-scale firms engaged in "apparel production excluding shoes" in the country had concentrated in Tehran province (Ostān-e Tehrān) as of 1991 (Markaz-e Āmār-e Īrān 1992, hasht-shānzdah).

It was also reported that 287 large-scale apparel-producing firms were operating in Tehran province as of 1998 (Sāzmān-e Modīrīyat va Bar-nāme-rīzī-ye Ostān-e Tehrān 2000, 348), equivalent to 70% of the total large-scale apparel-producing firms operating in the country at the time (Markaz-e Āmār-e Īrān 2000/01, 267).

Moreover, as described later, Iran Textile Exporters' Association (Ettehādīye-ye Toulīd-konande-gān va Sāder-konande-gān-e Sanāye'-e Nassājī va Pūshāk-e Īrān, hereafter ITEA) announced that approximately 250–300 large-scale apparel-producing firms were operating in Tehran province in 2010 (Iwasaki 2010, 1). This was far in excess of the figure regarding the whole country, as reported by MAI at the time. Therefore, Tehran province (or perhaps Tehran city) has presumably been the biggest center in the country, at least so far as large-scale apparel firms are concerned.

The same conclusion cannot be reached with regard to small-scale firms with fewer than 10 workers because conclusive statistics are not readily available. But the author's fieldwork has determined, without any doubt, that numerous tiny firms have been swarming thick as clouds in Tehran city.

Some representative places in Tehran can be named as apparel-producing centers home to small-scale firms, for example, Jomhūrī-ye Eslāmī Street in south Tehran and Bāzār-e Āhan-gar-hā Street in the Tehran Bazaar area. For some large-scale firms, only the offices remain in the center while their factories operate in a suburb like Karaj. But most firms operate using a room in a multitenant building crowded in the above-mentioned streets. Although the accurate number of small-scale firms based in Tehran is unknown, at the end of 1990 s, one could see in those areas more than a thousand small-scale firms side by side, generating loud machinery noise. Many small-scale firm owners often pointed out in interviews that it was quite important for the firm to be located in Tehran from the perspectives of raw materials procurement and market access.

The aforementioned data and findings reveal that Tehran definitely constitutes the foremost apparel-producing center in Iran; consequently, Tehran is a very informative and representative survey site for observing the characteristics of industrial organization in Iran's apparel industry.

3.2 Patterns of Apparel-Producing Firms Based on Interviews in 1998

First, let us classify the firms in Tehran's apparel-producing center according to certain indicators to enable an investigation of their state of organization. The author conducted a detailed interview survey in November 1998. The interviewees were private apparel firms selected on the basis of firm scale in cooperation with the Association of Iran Textile Industries (Anjoman-e Sanāye'-e Nassājī-ye Īrān) (see Table 3.1).

A total of 14 firms were interviewed during this round. Two firms (Firm B and Firm D) out of the 14 that had engaged in apparel-producing until some years ago had stopped operations and became specialized in fabric weaving at the time of interviews. Another firm (Firm JB) had also stopped producing apparel for the domestic market. Interview topics included conditions of the latest period when the informant firms were producing apparel products for the domestic market.

In line with some indicators that should be considered for our discussion, these 14 firms are divided into different groups.

3.2.1 *Firm Scale*

The first indicator is firm scale. As mentioned earlier, Iran's government offices, such as MAI and the Ministry of Industry, conventionally divide manufacturing firms operating in various fields into two categories on the basis of number of workers, namely "large-scale firms" with more than 10 workers and "small-scale firm" with fewer than 10 workers. This way of division has a certain utility in its local context since Iran's private manufacturing firms—including apparel firms—are, in general, quite small in scale (see Chap. 2).

According to the division, the 14 interview subject firms were classified as follows: 10 large-scale firms and 4 small-scale firms. Of the 10 large-scale firms, two had just 10 workers and might therefore be classified as small-scale firms from the viewpoint of their business status. The other eight large-scale firms can be considered relatively large compared with the distribution of apparel firm scale at the time. However, despite the insufficient informant responses, it became clear even with some firms' fragmentary data that the more the number of workers increases, the more a firm's business volume tends to expand.

3.2.2 *Degree of Reliance on Outsourcing*

The second indicator is the degree of reliance on outsourcing. The interviewed firms can be divided into three groups according to this criterion. The first group consists

Table 3.1 List of informant firms in interview survey 1998

Firm code	Product	Number of workers	Outsourcing part	Product planning	Sales channel	Date of interview
RG	Children's clothes	250	Basically none	In-house	*Bonak-dār*	15 Nov
Z	Children's clothes, sportswear	183	None	In-house designer	*Bonak-dār*	16 Nov
JG	Denim jeans, shirts	120	Weaving	The director	Own shop	24 Nov
G	Woolen clothes	60	Weaving	The director, staff	Own shop	24 Nov
JB	Knitwear for women, men and children	50	Knitting	The director, staff	*Bonak-dār*	19 Nov
S	Children's clothes	30	Weaving, printing	The director, staff	Retailer	15 Nov
B	Velvet, women's coat	23	None	In-house	*Bonak-dār*	14 Nov
F	Synthetic yarn, knitwear for women	20	Embroidering	The director	Retailer, *bonak-dār*	22 Nov
BJ	Men's shirts	10	Weaving, embroidering, collar	The director	Retailer, *bonak-dār*	14 Nov
D	Children's clothes	10	Embroidering, rarely sewing	The director, staff	*Bonak-dār*	21 Nov
T	Specialized embroiderer	8	None			22 Nov
R	Children's and women's clothes	5	Weaving, embroidering, printing	The director	*Bonak-dār*	18 Nov
N	Men's clothes	3	All except knitting	The director	*Bonak-dār*	25 Nov
FI	Girls' clothes, men's pants	2	All except knitting	The director	*Bonak-dār*	25 Nov

Source Prepared by the author

of the firms that carry out the entire apparel manufacturing process (cutting, printing, sewing, finishing, and so on) in their own factories. The second group consists of firms that outsource only value-adding processes, such as embroidery and printing, to specialist outside firms. The last group consists of firms that consign all manufacturing processes to outside firms.

Out of the informants in this survey, six firms belong to the first group, five to the second group, and two to the third group (the one remaining firm is a specialized embroiderer). The firms in the respective groups resembled each other in firm scale. In other words, the larger the firm's scale (business volume), the lower was its reliance on outsourcing. On the other hand, smaller firms were outsourcing considerable parts of manufacturing process to outside firms.

3.2.3 Product Planning Methods

The third indicator is the method used in the product planning process. Two points were investigated in this survey to determine how apparel-producing firms cooperated with distributors, namely (1) if whether the firms accept orders for certain product models from wholesalers or retailers before production, (2) in what ways the firms undertake planning for new products.

Two types of firms were observed as a result of interviews. One type produces a certain model according to a foreign distributor's detailed order regarding design and color. The other was never accepted any distributor's order before production. Needless to say, only the exporting firms were the first type. But such firms were also of the second type for the domestic market. No firm produced apparel goods for the domestic market on the basis of order from the distributor before production. In short, all the informant firms were producing apparel goods for the domestic market based on their own market assessment and not on orders from distributors.

3.2.4 Market Development

The fourth indicator is the choice of distribution channel. As mentioned above, the interviewed firms were producing goods based on their own market assessments. In what way did each firm circulate their products in the market?

There were two types of firms in this regard. The first type of firm placed products on sale on consignment through wholesalers called *bonak-dār*, and the majority of firms employed this route. The second type of firm sold products through their own shop or familiar retailer without contacting *bonak-dār*s. There were two firms of the latter type in the survey, both of which were large-scale firms.

This approach elucidated that most of the interviewed firms consigned finished products for sale and barely made contact with retailers who had more information about end users.

The findings from the 1998 fieldwork survey can be summarized as follows: (1) the larger firms relied less on outsourcing, (2) firms carried out their own product planning, and (3) few of the interviewees had direct relations with retailers.

These characteristics seemed to persist thereafter, and the industry has always been separated into a few large-scale firms operating amongst a great number of petty independent enterprises that are not integrated into the production streams of any of the large-scale firms.

3.3 Apparel-Producing Firms in Tehran: Overview of Results from the Questionnaire Survey 2010

In 2010, the author conducted a much larger scale questionnaire survey (and a supplementary interview survey) in Tehran.[1]

The surveys intended to investigate more concrete and detailed patterns of Iran's apparel-producing firms, focusing on firms operating in Tehran. In circumstances where the apparel firms were operating independently without being organized into a vertical (or even horizontal) production chain with other firms, how do they carry out the production and sales of their products?

To answer this question, the author conducted a questionnaire survey in 2010. The following is an overview of the results from this survey, with qualitative data added from interviews conducted by the author with concerned interviewees during 2008–2011 (see Table 3.2).

3.3.1 Survey Design

The survey of firms was conducted using two main methods: a questionnaire survey and supplementary interviews with selected apparel firms. The subjects of the survey were large-scale apparel firms employing more than 10 workers whose main office (or factory) is located in Tehran Province.

Questionnaires were distributed to 250 large-scale apparel firms, which were almost all such firms[2] in Tehran Province at the time of the survey. The questionnaires were distributed by the ITEA, a collaborator of the research project.

---

[1]The questionnaire survey was organized and conducted by the author as a part of a joint research project of the Need-based Area Studies Program "Middle East within Asia" (Hitotsubashi University) and IDE. Practical support in conducting the survey was provided by the Faculty of World Studies, University of Tehran. This section was a discussion paper of IDE (Iwasaki 2012).

[2]The reliability and timeliness of Iran's official statistical data are problematic. For the apparel industry, the data gathered by the ITEA, the industry's private trade association, is considered to reflect the reality of the industry in a more accurate and timely manner than the data published by the MAI. Therefore, this study used the data of the ITEA, which showed that there were about 250–300 large-scale apparel firms located in Tehran Province during the time of the survey, although the number fluctuates seasonally. The number 250 for the number of firms selected to be surveyed is based on the average number of large-scale firms that the ITEA estimates are located in Tehran Province.

Table 3.2 List of main informants in interview surveys 2008–2011

Firm code	Category of business	Location of firm	Number of workers in producing firm	Number of members of organization	Date of interview
SHC	Wholesale of children's clothes	Jomhūrī St.	/	/	30 Oct 2008, 19 Apr 2011
FF	Wholesale of women's clothes	Tehran Bazaar	/	/	2 Nov 2008, 11 Dec 2010, 20 Nov 2011
Iran textile exporters association	Trade association in private sector	/	/	400	3 Nov 2008, 12 Feb 2011
J	*Namāyande* in textile	/	/	/	9 Nov 2008
H	Production and retail of men's clothes	Motahharī St.	700	/	17 Aug 2009
G2	Production and retail of men's clothes	Abbās ābād	550	/	14 Nov 2010
M	Production, wholesale and retail of men's clothes	Mīrdāmād St.	150	/	16 Nov 2010
KTI	Production of casual clothes (subcontractor of foreign firm)	Karaj	120	/	16 Nov 2010
MK	Wholesale of knitwear	Jomhūrī St.	/	/	1 Dec 2010, 28 Nov 2011
TG	Wholesale of knitwear	Tehran Bazaar	/	/	4 Dec 2010
S2	Wholesale of knitwear	Tehran Bazaar	/	/	4 Dec 2010
J2	Wholesale of women's underwear	Tehran Bazaar	/	/	11 Dec 2010
JD	Wholesale of women's clothes and accessories	Tehran Bazaar	/	/	26 Nov 2011
IR	Wholesale of women's clothes	Jomhūrī St.	/	/	16 Jan 2011

(continued)

Table 3.2 (continued)

Firm code	Category of business	Location of firm	Number of workers in producing firm	Number of members of organization	Date of interview
Trade union production and vender garment Tehran	Trade association in private sector	/	/	20,000	18 Jan 2011
N2	Production of women's clothes	Jomhūrī St.	14	/	30 Jan 2011
FZ	Production of women's knitwear	Jomhūrī St.	12	/	26 Feb 2011
JZ	Wholesale of women's clothes	Tehran Bazaar	/	/	26 Apr 2011

Source Prepared by the author

Some of the surveyed firms were members of the association. Out of the 250 firms receiving the questionnaire, 127 firms had responded by May 2010, giving a response rate of 50.8%.[3]

The questionnaire asked for general information about the firm and about production, capital, financial resources, human capital, supply chains, customers, cooperation with other firms, and marketing methods.[4]

Along with the questionnaire survey, supplementary interviews with several firms and their related trade associations were also conducted by the author during 2009–2011.[5] The firms interviewed were not necessarily ones who participated in the questionnaire survey.

3.3.2 *Main Findings*

3.3.2.1 Location and Scale of Large-Scale Firms

A rough pattern of the 127 firms that responded can be drawn from their location, year of establishment, and number of workers.

When asked about the location of their main office, most firms answered that they were in Tehran city, particularly in the 11th and 12th districts (Fig. 3.1). These two

[3]For the collected results, see Iwasaki (2010).

[4]The content of the questionnaire was the same as that of other questionnaire surveys implemented in Egypt and Jordan as a part of an above-mentioned joint research project by Hitotsubashi University.

[5]The author stayed in Tehran from June 2009 until June 2011 as a visiting researcher at University of Tehran. The interview surveys were carried out periodically during the author's stay.

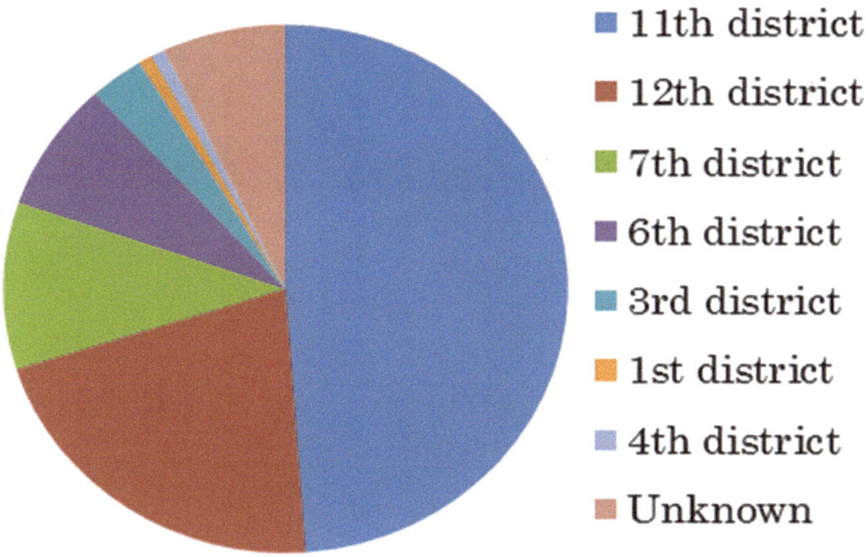

Fig. 3.1 Location of the firms. *Note* City of Tehran is divided into 22 administrative districts. *Source* Iwasaki (2010: 3)

districts are contiguous and located south of Enqelāb-e Eslāmī Street, which runs east–west in the city center. This area has some well-known business quarters where many *bonak-dār*s have their shops, and consequently many related industrial firms are also concentrated here. The results of the questionnaire survey confirmed this.

More than 80% of the firms were established after 1350 (1971/72) (Fig. 3.2). On the whole, it seems that the firms operating for more than 20 years are large-scale firms and are maintaining Iran's apparel production.

To the question about the number of workers, 55% of the 127 firms answered "10–49 workers" (Fig. 3.3). This means that more than half of the 127 large-scale firms employ fewer than 50 workers. It needs to be mentioned that 32 firms employed fewer than 10 workers, although the survey was conducted on the assumption that the firms under investigation were large-scale firms with more than 10 workers. This result shows that the number of workers is fluid, and firms sometimes may exclude their family members from their count of number of workers employed. Whatever the case, we can see that on the whole, Iranian apparel firms are petty enterprises.

More than 30% of the surveyed firms answered that "more than half" of their workforce consisted of women; this includes firms reporting that more than 70% of their workers were women (Fig. 3.4). This reveals that the popular impression about the low level of participation by women workers in manufacturing in Iran compared with a country such as Turkey is incorrect. Nevertheless, the 1998 interview survey showed that few women were working in such firms. This indicates that the large number of women working in apparel firms is a relatively recent phenomenon.

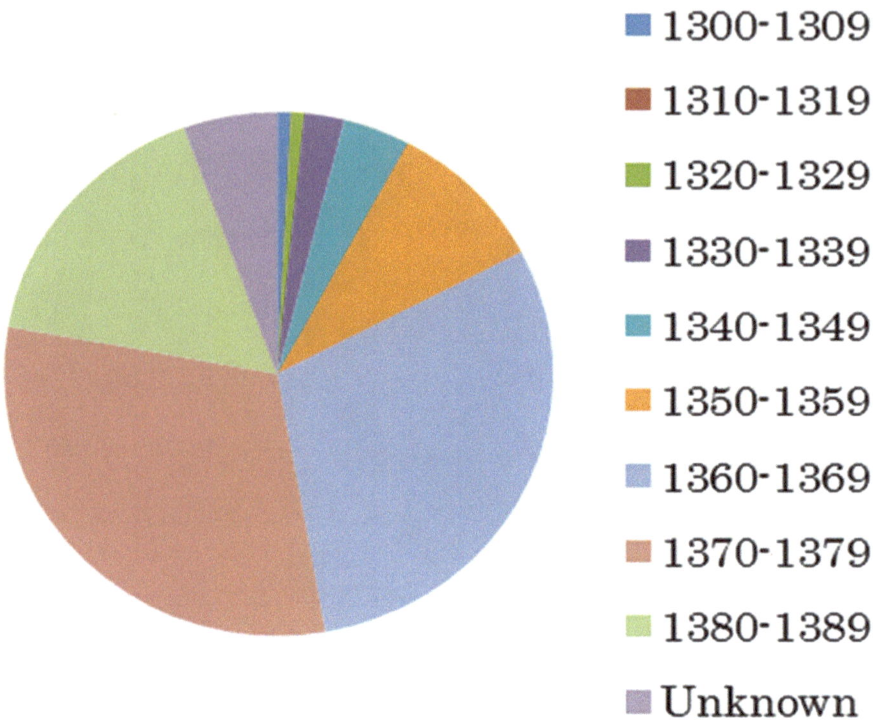

Fig. 3.2 Year of establishment of the firms. *Note* Based on Iranian calendar, 1300 corresponds to March 1921–March 1922. *Source* Iwasaki (2010: 3)

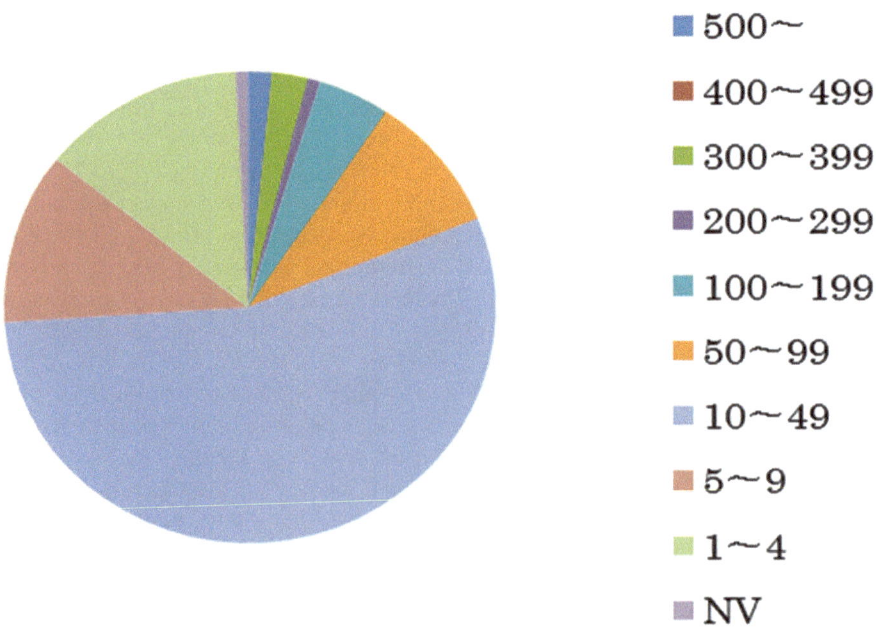

Fig. 3.3 Number of workers of the firms. *Source* Iwasaki (2010: 4)

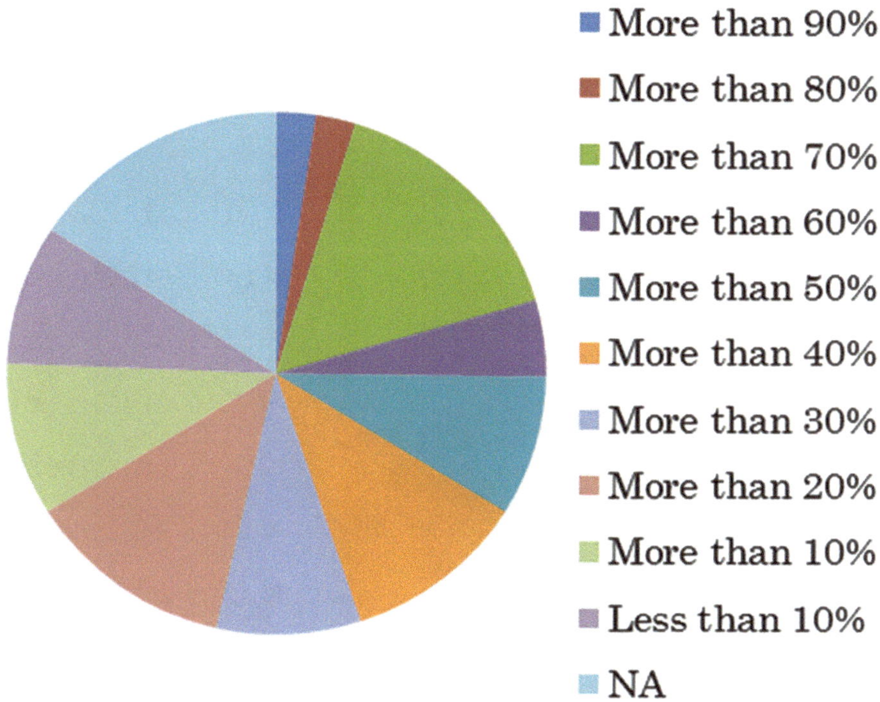

Fig. 3.4 Ratio of female workers of the firms. *Source* Iwasaki (2010: 6)

3.3.2.2 Supply Chain Characteristics

Iranian manufacturing, regardless of business type, relies on imported raw materials and machinery. The responses of the surveyed firms to the question about the ratio of imported raw materials to the total volume of raw materials consumed by the firms ranged from "less than 10%" to "100%" (Fig. 3.5). The most frequent answer was "more than 20% and less than 30%;" however, one-fourth answered "more than 50%," including two firms that answered "100%." Fabrics and yarns were imported mainly from China and Turkey.

To the question about the ratio of imported machinery and spare parts, 75% of the firms answered "more than 70%," including 30% that answered "100%" (Fig. 3.6). This result again shows the Iranian apparel industry's high degree of dependency on imported machinery and spare parts. The main suppliers of these imports were Japan and Germany.

The notable point here is that the most common answer to procurement method of imported raw materials and machinery was "import directly" (Figs. 3.7 and 3.8).

As already mentioned in Chap. 2, after the Revolution in 1979 and the subsequent series of crises that included internal disorder, the Iran–Iraq War, and Iran's isolation from the international community, the government introduced a very strict

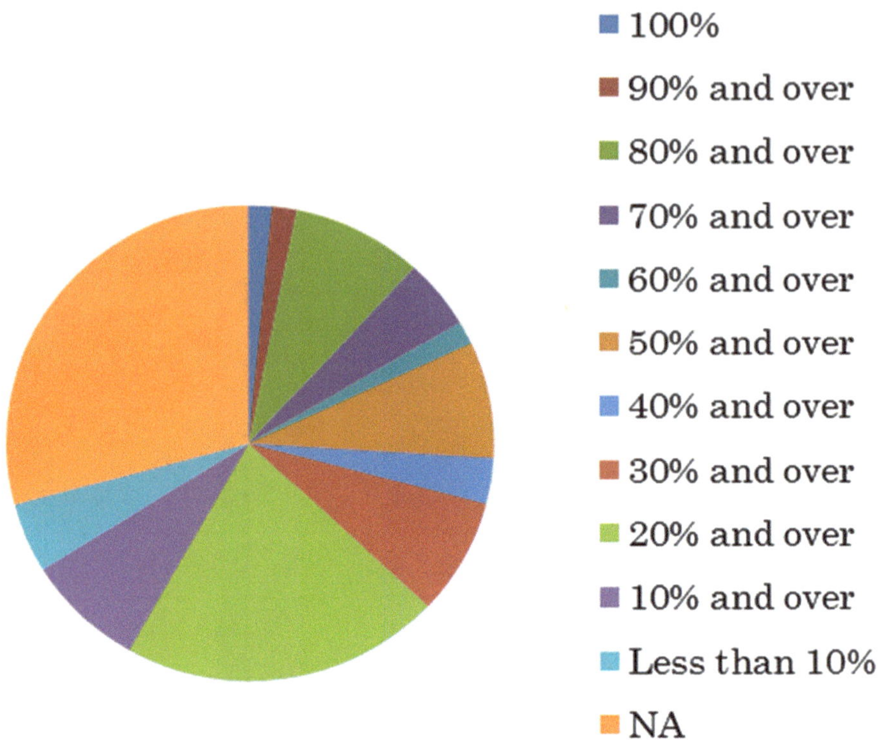

Fig. 3.5 Ratio of imported raw materials. *Source* Iwasaki (2010: 9)

import restriction policy combined with exchange rate controls. Foreign currency allocation was strictly controlled, an import permission system was introduced, and non-producers were, in principle, forbidden to import goods from abroad, even though Iranian manufacturing had relied heavily on imported raw materials and machinery since the Pahlavi era. Consequently, domestic producers were required to procure foreign goods on their own without help from international traders.

Under these severe circumstances, some large-scale firms set up their own in-house public relations section, but this approach was rather exceptional. Many firms outsourced the procurement of machinery and raw materials as well as imported goods through an intermediary called a "*namāyande*" (this aspect will be discussed in detail in Chap. 4). This type of agent, however, did not have any right to buy foreign goods personally; his only role was to find an opposite party for the transaction and bring about the signing of a contract. Therefore, it seems that even small-scale firms who had no real staff nonetheless accumulated a certain amount of know-how in affairs pertaining to importing.

The restriction policies were eased greatly from 2000, and now even non-producers can participate in importing. Firms are also able to procure imported raw materials from the domestic market. In an interview, Firm G2 commented:

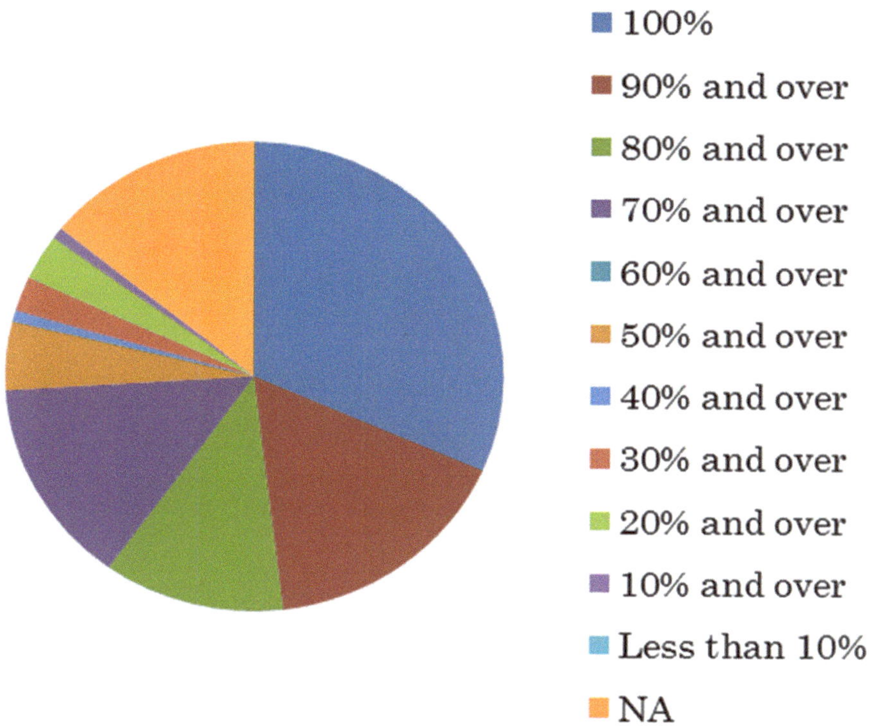

Fig. 3.6 Ratio of imported machinery and spare parts. *Source* Iwasaki (2010: 11)

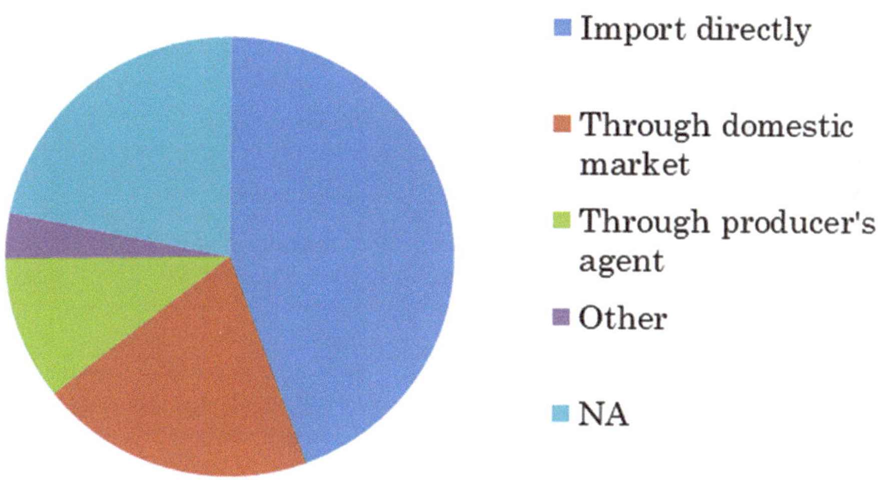

Fig. 3.7 Way of procurement of imported raw materials. *Note* A multiple response question. *Source* Iwasaki (2010: 10)

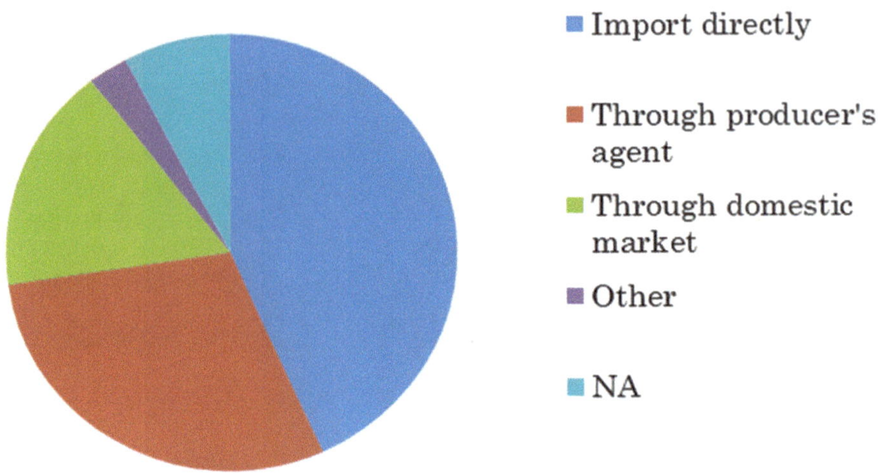

Fig. 3.8 Way of procurement of imported machinery and spare parts. *Note* A multiple response question. *Source* Iwasaki (2010: 12)

> There is no problem in procurement of raw materials at the moment; (troublesome official procedures have been) greatly eased.[6]

A very interesting point concerning importation is that half of the firms who answered "import directly" about their method of procuring imports (mentioned above) answered the question about who intermediates transactions between their firm and foreign producers of machinery and spare parts by saying "Iranian broker," which is the same method used during the time of the restriction policies (Fig. 3.9). This shows there is still room for "*namāyande*" to work as agents for firms in procuring machinery that requires technical knowledge. Firm KTI acknowledged in an interview that the "*namāyande*" system of intermediating in the import of raw materials and charging a commission without becoming a party in the transaction still functions in the apparel industry:

> Yes, there are ones who charge commission, in some items imported.[7]

On the other hand, regarding the question concerning the import of raw materials such as fabrics and yarns, many firms answered "there is no intermediary" (Fig. 3.10). In other words, firms purchase these goods directly from foreign producers. Firms indicated China as the main supplier of these products. Huge wholesale markets called 'Specialized Market' have developed in that country in recent years as places where Chinese local producers have opened their own stores selling their manufactured products to domestic merchants as well as foreign

---

[6]Interviewed on November 14, 2010.

[7]Interviewed on November 16, 2010.

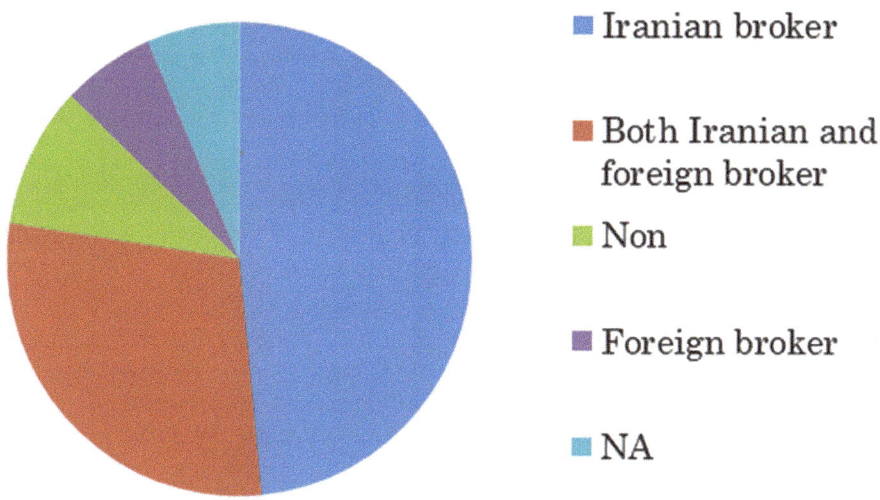

Fig. 3.9 Mediator of machinery and spare parts import. *Source* Iwasaki (2010: 12)

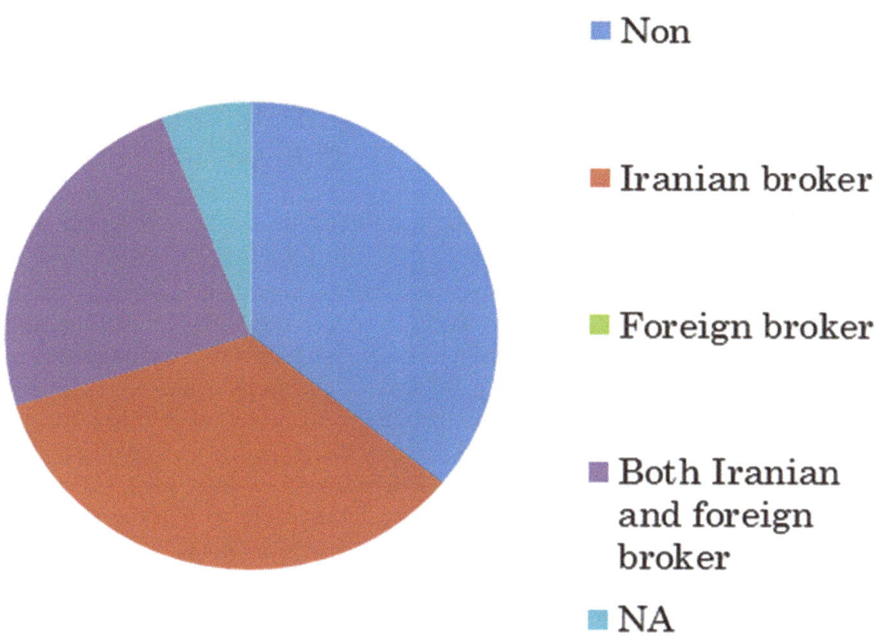

Fig. 3.10 Mediator of raw materials import. *Source* Iwasaki (2010: 10)

buyers. There are also well-known markets among Iranian buyers in Turkey, which is close to Iran both linguistically and geographically. The survey results show that the existence of such markets make it much easier for firms to procure raw materials.

As stated above, Iran's large-scale apparel firms depend greatly on imported raw materials and machinery, which they purchase directly from markets abroad. Although the role of the "*namāyande*" has grown more limited as a result, it seems that intermediaries rich in experience and knowledge are still active in highly technical fields such as machinery.

3.3.2.3 Cooperation with Other Firms

Iranian small-scale apparel firms with fewer than 10 workers tend not to cooperate with each other and have barely developed mutual vertical relationships running from production through distribution. The 1998 interview survey showed that even relatively large-scale firms at that time seldom outsourced work, instead performing every manufacturing process by themselves. In the present survey, regarding the question about outsourcing a part of the manufacturing process, more than half of respondent firms answered "yes" (Fig. 3.11). The process they most frequently outsourced was sewing, followed by weaving and embroidering.

However, about 60% of the firms answering "yes" to the above question made temporary contracts with contractors (Fig. 3.12), indicating that their relationships were not necessarily regular. Firms KTI and FZ confirmed this in interviews.[8] According to Firm N, handwork like sewing on accessories is mainly done by Afghan workers in Iran:

> An Afghan comes to get some work and takes it back home. A person in charge assigns the work to his family members.[9]

This comment may show that the domestic labor market for contract work is divided by nationality.

On the other hand, in response to the question of whether they do piecework for other companies, less than 30% of the firms answered "yes" (Fig. 3.13). Moreover, in response to the question about their relationships with other companies, most firms answered "temporary." It is plausible to think that they do piecework for other companies in the same business only when their friends are not able to manage.

The survey indicates that outsourcing has become more common compared with how it was in 1998, when most firms undertook every manufacturing process by themselves, although the relationships between firms remain as weak as ever. This shows the Iranian inclination in business is to avoid regular contact with other firms and remain far from contemplating capital alliances.

A very rare case, however, was found in the interviews, where the Iranian apparel firm, designated KTI, operated entirely as the contractor of a foreign company. This firm used to supply their products to the domestic market but quit this work completely and became a contractor for an Italian apparel firm. By the

---

[8]Interviewed on February 26, 2011.

[9]Interviewed on January 30, 2011.

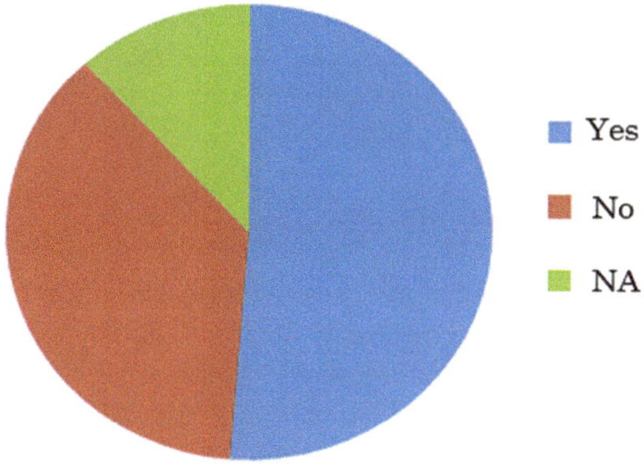

Fig. 3.11 Outsourcing. *Source* Iwasaki (2010: 16)

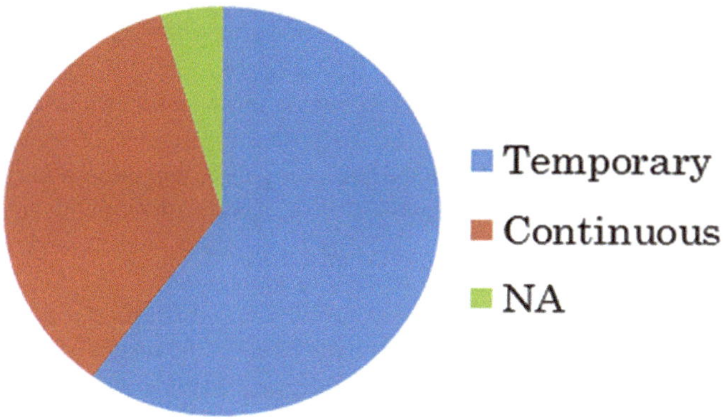

Fig. 3.12 Relationship with outside suppliers. *Source* Iwasaki (2010: 16)

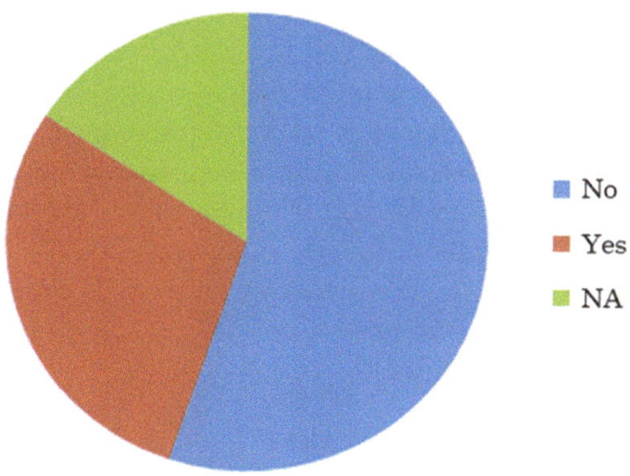

Fig. 3.13 Piecework for other company. *Source* Iwasaki (2010: 16)

time of the 1990s survey, European and Japanese apparel firms had concluded that they could rely only on Turkey among the Middle East countries as a place for contractors. "The circumstances are changing," said Firm KTI.[10]

3.3.2.4 Main Customers and Markets

As stated before, Iranian small-scale apparel firms with fewer than 10 workers generally sell their products by consignment to *bonak-dār*s whose shops are located in several areas of Tehran. These *bonak-dār* shops are well-known all over the country. Tehran serves as the hub where products from all parts of the country are traded and where wholesalers and retailers from the provinces come to meet, which makes the city the biggest trading center for apparel products in Iran. Even small-scale firms are able to sell their products all over the country through the *bonak-dār*s (for more details, see Chap. 5).

Regarding exports, in response to the question about the ratio of the firm's products that are exported, 7% of the surveyed firms answered "more than 50%" while four firms answered "100%" (Fig. 3.14). More than 60%, however, gave no answer. These results suggest that even many large-scale firms do little or no exporting. For the firms that do export, Iraq was the biggest buyer, followed by Germany, Afghanistan, and Azerbaijan. Excluding Germany, neighboring countries were the biggest export markets. Two of these, Iraq and Afghanistan, have seen their domestic industries ruined by war. Both countries have a large demand for foreign goods and are big buyers of Iranian products.

As pointed out above, many large-scale apparel firms produce solely for the domestic market. How do these firms secure buyers? In response to the question about the firm's main customer, the most frequent answer was "domestic wholesaler" (Fig. 3.15), and 80% of these wholesalers were based in Tehran. This is a clear reference to the *bonak-dār*. According to the Trade Union Production and Vendor Garment Tehran (Ettehādīye-ye Senf-e Toulīd-konande-gān va Forūshande-gān-e Pūshāk-e Tehrān), the number of *bonak-dār*s in Tehran city as of 2011 was about 4000,[11] which did not differ from the last survey in the late 1990s.

Nevertheless, it became clear in the interviews that some firms (Firm H, Firm KTI, and Firm G2) had established their own markets without relying on *bonak-dār*s, who had caused difficulties for these firms' business, for instance, by taking a long time to clear transactions and posing a nonpayment risk. On the other hand, one large-scale firm (Firm N) said they appreciated the *bonak-dār*s' selling power, remarking that "it won't pay without *bonak-dār*s."[12] On the whole, the larger the firm, the stronger its tendency to seek out its own channels separate from the *bonak-dār*s for selling its products.

[10]Interviewed on November 16, 2010.

[11]Interviewed on January 18, 2011.

[12]Interviewed on January 30, 2011.

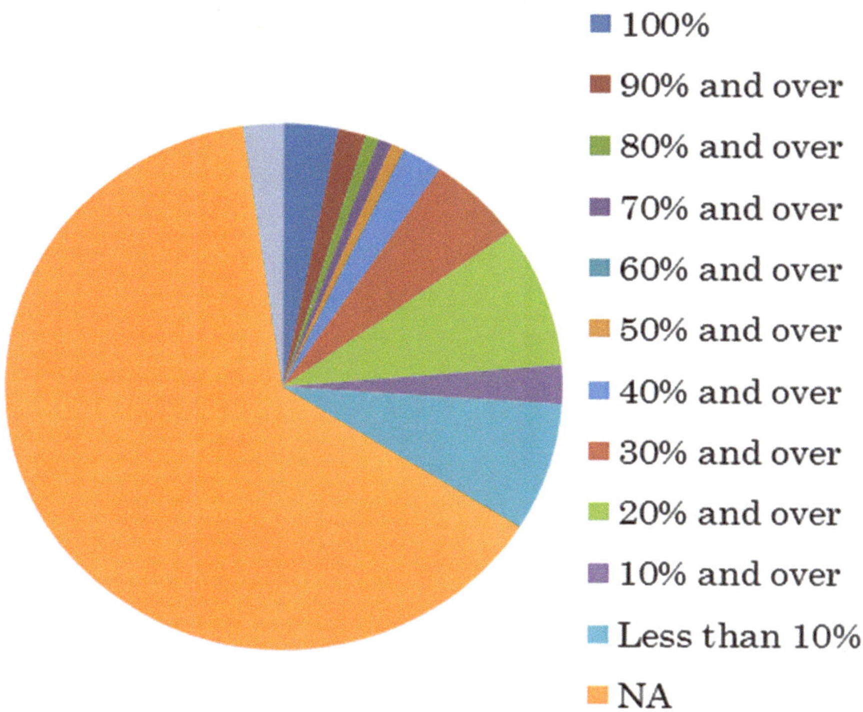

Fig. 3.14 Ratio of exported products. *Source* Iwasaki (2010: 15)

This is evidenced by the fact that the percentage of respondents who answered "domestic retailers" came soon after the most frequent answer to the same question. In this regard, large-scale firms differ very much from small-scale firms with fewer than 10 workers that have neither established their own brands nor have their own marketing staff and, therefore, must consign nearly all of their products to *bonak-dār*s for sale. Approximately 90% of the aforementioned "domestic retailers" are also located in Tehran.

In terms of domestic retailing, 60% of the firms answered "yes" to the question about setting up their own shops. It is likely that the "domestic retailers" in Fig. 3.15 include the firms' own shops. By selling their products to final consumers in Tehran, large-scale apparel firms are advertising their brands to the people while at the same time making the city, the biggest trade center for apparel goods in Iran, into a source of new fashion.

Regarding sales of products that involved mainly domestic wholesalers (*bonak-dār*s) and retailers, the survey clearly showed that the time allowed for clearing a transaction grew and the main means of clearance was "cash" (Fig. 3.16). The 1998 interview survey showed that the normal term of clearance ranged from a few months to up to one year. This reflects the fact that transactions between firms and *bonak-dār*s took the form of commission selling, and the amount of payment was

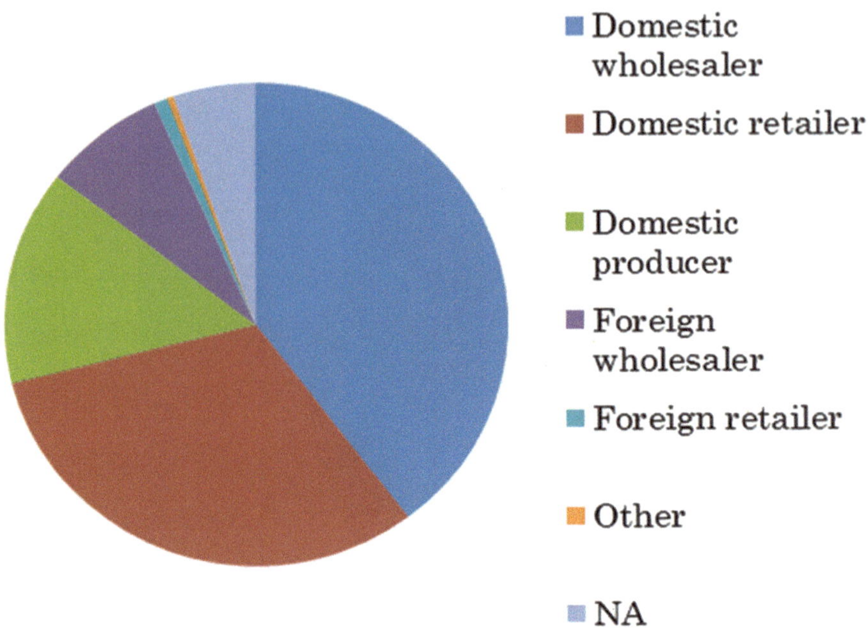

Fig. 3.15 Type of buyer. *Note* A multiple response question. *Source* Iwasaki (2010: 13)

not settled until the end of the season. The long delay in the clearance of payments for transactions is clearly a financial burden on firms who need to cover their production costs. Considering the lack of diverse domestic distribution channels and the strong selling power of the *bonak-dār*s, sales through these wholesalers seems to be the best choice at the moment for Iran's small-scale apparel firms.

3.3.2.5 Marketing

Looking at the marketing strategies used by apparel firms, the Iranian apparel industry in general rarely invests in the development of new products or differentiation from other products owing to small size of the majority of its firms.

For the numerous small-scale firms, it is safe to maintain business by producing lower cost products that imitate those other companies' best selling products. For large-scale firms, products have often been no more than ideas borrowed from European and American fashion magazines with some tiny alterations. Iran's isolation in international society and the government's interception of information after the revolution has slowed the effect of foreign fashion trends, which has left Iran's domestic apparel and fashion market immature.

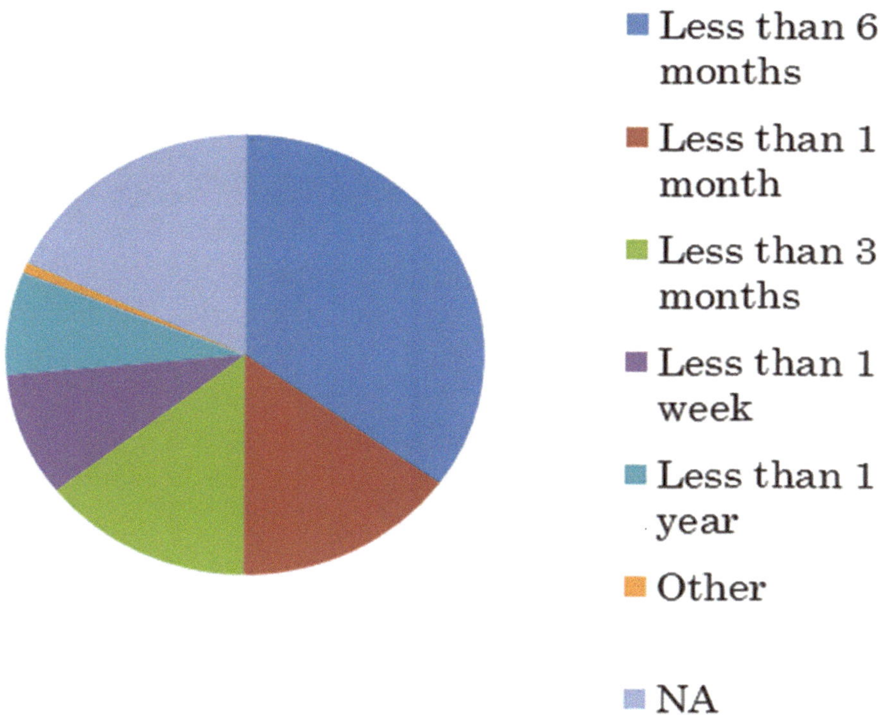

Fig. 3.16 Term for clearance with buyers. *Note* Some made multiple responses. *Source* Iwasaki (2010: 14)

In recent years, however, some large-scale firms have been making efforts to hasten the adoption of current Western fashions and reinterpret them according to domestic consumers' tastes to produce original products. Reflecting this trend, more than half of the interviewed firms answered "yes" (Fig. 3.17) to the question about setting up a market research section in the firm.

Moreover, to the question about the source of market information, the most frequent answer, given by 60% of the firms, was "customers" (Fig. 3.18), which contrasted with small firms, who normally had no idea to whom the *bonak-dār*s sold their products.

It is plausible that many of the large-scale firms are able to analyze the reactions of their consumers as 60% of them have their own shops, as mentioned above. Only 20% of the firms answered that they obtain information from the *bonak-dār*s. It seems the reciprocation of information between *bonak-dār*s and producers is quite limited, as it is with the small firms. In an interview, Firm N2 rejected the possibility of communication between the two before the production of a product, remarking:

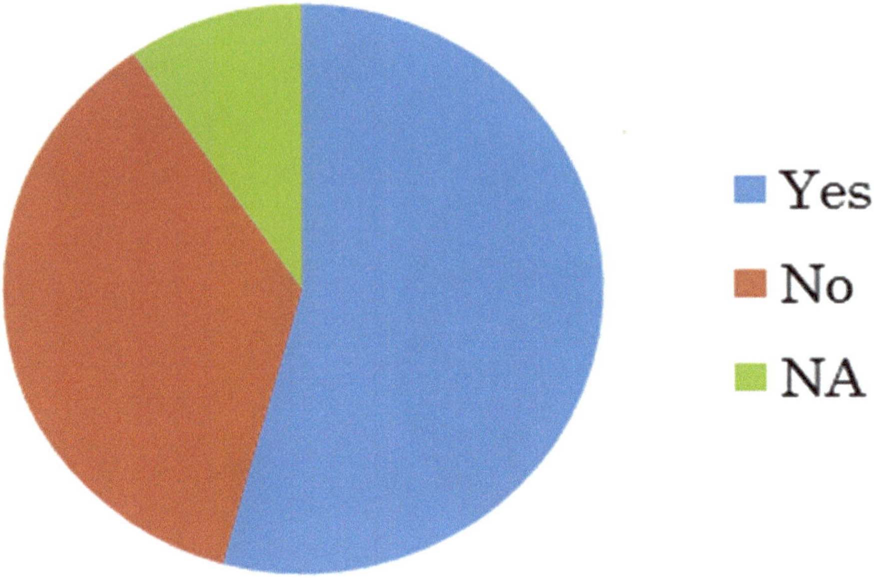

Fig. 3.17 Have a marketing research section. *Source* Iwasaki (2010: 18)

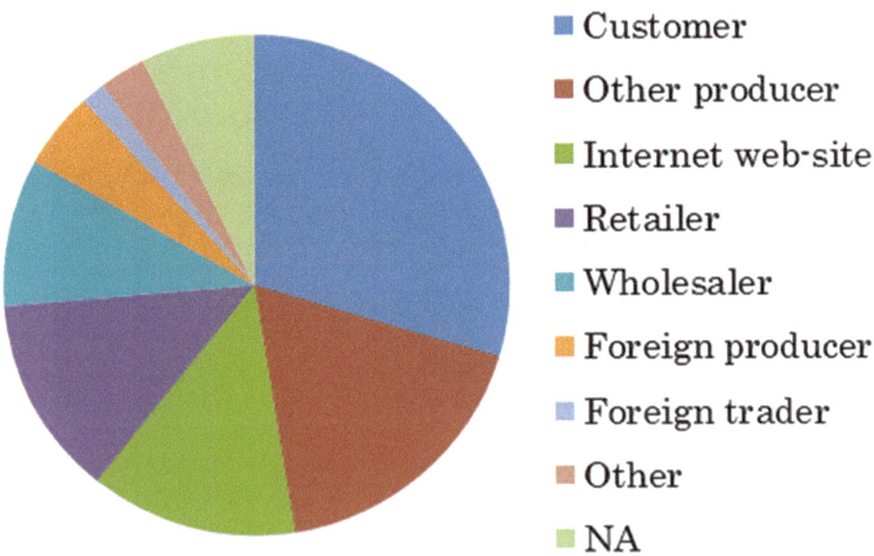

Fig. 3.18 Source of market information. *Note* A multiple response question. *Source* Iwasaki (2010: 18)

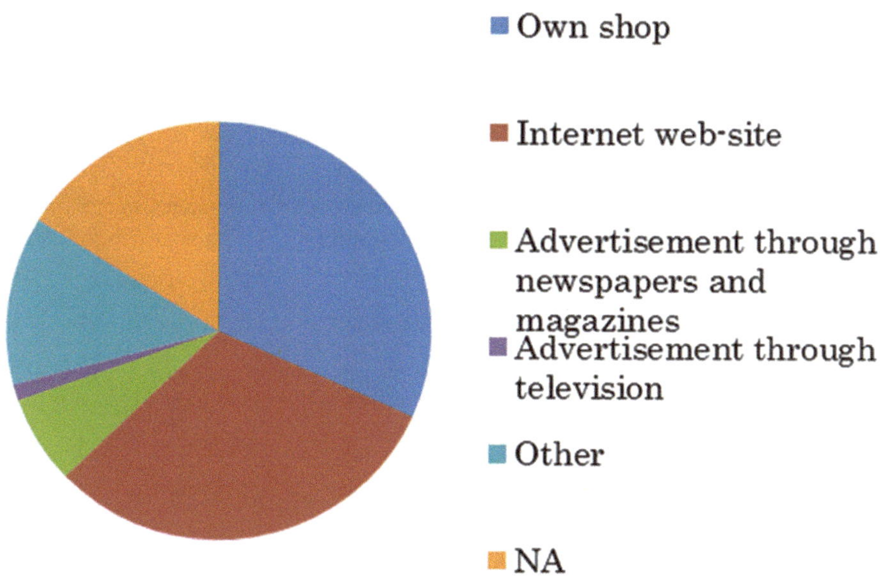

Fig. 3.19 Means of sales promotion. *Note* A multiple response question. *Source* Iwasaki (2010: 19)

> If the design is good, the *bonak-dār*s will reply. They [the products] will sell well. In Iran it is difficult to secure orders before that.[13]

Firm H, which sells all of its products through its own shops, said:

> The information they [*bonak-dār*s] have is of no use for us. We know who our customers are and what they require. We do not intend to make clothes for everyone.[14]

The fundamental marketing strategy of large-scale and successful firms seems to be producing differentiated products for the differentiated market.

In response to the question about the firm's main means of promoting sales, most firms answered "own shop," followed by "Internet site" (Fig. 3.19). It is not very profitable for firms to sell their differentiated products through consignment in the *bonak-dār*s' shops, where products from a large number of unspecified producers are displayed together without any distinction. Therefore, many large-scale apparel firms in Iran regard their own shops and advertising as indispensable for branding the firm and its products.

As indicated above, the large-scale apparel firms that have managed to maintain good performance are the ones targeting their consumers and proceeding with product differentiation to create original markets. However, when several trade associations were asked in interviews about the interest that Iran's large-scale

[13]Interviewed on January 30, 2011.

[14]Interviewed on August 17, 2009.

apparel firms have in foreign markets, all of them denied the existence of any such interest, emphasizing instead the extensive size of the domestic market. Expressing this view, one interviewee commented:

> The domestic market accounts for the major part of profits. The market here is promising [for business].[15]

The ITEA pointed out the backwardness of the business practices in the Iranian apparel industry and was skeptical about the possibility of its expansion into foreign markets. One Association employee commented:

> The business attitude for foreign markets differs greatly from the one for the domestic market. These are completely dissimilar [areas of] business. Deadline must be met; prices must not be changed; [firms] must keep up with the latest fashion.... They may lose their market to others after years of effort. Therefore, not everyone can deal in the export business.[16]

3.3.2.6 Summary of Questionnaire and Supplementary Interview Surveys During 2009–2011

As has been demonstrated, many of the large-scale apparel firms in Iran are based in Tehran and have been in business for approximately 20 years. They have solid businesses with regular customers, but in general, they have hesitated to expand the size of their firms. Since the relaxation of restrictions imposed in the 1990s on the procurement of raw materials, the results of the survey show that the firms have developed new channels of procurement, although they depend to a considerable degree on imported raw materials and machinery.

As mentioned in Chap. 2, large-scale firms have managed to maintain their output even following the rapid increase in imports since 2000, although the number of firms has decreased. Low-priced products such as those from China have basically not been rivals for such large-scale firms, although the inflow of foreign branded products hit Iranian firms heavily. As a result, the outsourcing of some manufacturing processes was noted in the survey, which has never seen before in large-scale firms. This change indicates that competition with foreign companies has forced large-scale firms to reduce expenses, as has the recent increase in the costs of operating a business in Iran.

To maintain their market in the face of competition from foreign companies, some firms have invested in the differentiation of their products and building a brand name. At the same time, other companies sell their products by imitating foreign brands, although they have ability to produce results of sorts. This manifests a serious difficulty in Iran for firms to establish a brand name as well as the probable preference of high-income Iranian consumers for foreign brand products.

---

[15]Interviewed on January 18, 2011.

[16]Interviewed on February 12, 2011.

3.4 Typical Pattern of Firms

Through surveys conducted in Tehran in the 1990s and 2000s, the typical pattern of Iranian apparel-producing firms has been clarified. Their organizational characteristics lie in firm scale and the relationships among firms.

Although an overwhelming majority of apparel-producing firms is very small in scale, they are rarely involved in vertical integration with a large-scale firm. They often put out works to other small-scale firms but something like a joint-stock partnership has never been observed.

Large-scale firms also tend to avoid establishing strong ties with outside contractors in production. Although outsourcing has become more common than before, the relations between firms and contractors remain temporary and flexible. Due to the absence of industrial consolidation, large-scale firms remain relatively small as well, especially compared with highly integrated firms abroad.

On the whole, the very small size and independence of firms can be identified as extremely prominent features of the industrial organization of Iran's apparel-producing industry.

The actual production processes used by such small and independent apparel firms will be examined in the next chapter.

References

Iwasaki, Y. (2010). *Questionnaire survey on apparel firms in Iran 2010*. Middle East within Asia Research Report Series No. 11. Tokyo: Hitotsubashi University.

Iwasaki, Y. (2012). The business management strategy of Iran's large apparel firms: Overview of results from a questionnaire survey and interviews 2009–2011. Discussion Paper No.327. Japan: Institute of Developing Economies.

Markaz-e Āmār-e Īrān. (1992). *Nām va Neshānī-ye Kār-gāh-hā-ye Bozorg-e San'atī-ye Keshvar (The directory of large manufacturing firms in Iran)*. Tehrān.

Markaz-e Āmār-e Īrān. (2000/01). *Sāl-nāme-ye Āmārī-ye Keshvar 1378 (Iran statistical yearbook 1378)*. Tehrān.

Sāzmān-e Modīrīyat o Barnāme-rīzī -ye Ostān-e Tehrān. (2000). *Āmār-nāme-ye Ostān-e Tehrān Sāl-e 1378 (Statistics Data of Tehran Province 1378)*. Tehrān.

Chapter 4
The Apparel Production Process in Iran

Abstract Unlike Japan, Iran has no large-scale firm that organizes smaller contractors for actual production in the apparel-producing system. The procurement of raw materials and machinery serves as a crucial but weighty task for each firm, which operates independently, especially given the presence of rather strict import restrictions imposed by the government. The *namāyande* system functioned as a cure for this difficult situation encountered by small-scale firms. The lack of knowledge in firms for collecting and analyzing the information that a *namāyande* provided made him necessary for firms. Business management based on personal relationships is another factor making the *namāyande* a necessary player for firms, who seek to strengthen their external information channels by developing reliable relationships through extremely personal ties with their *namāyande* to survive in Iran's fluid business environment.

Keywords Work flow of apparel production · Procurement of machinery and raw materials · *Namāyande* system · Personal business relations

4.1 Process from Production to Sale

The previous chapter clarified the typical pattern of apparel-producing firms in Iran based on firsthand interviews and questionnaire surveys conducted by the author. Over the course of the interviews, the concrete process that firms used to produce apparel goods was also revealed. This chapter will discuss the flow of operations from the production to sale of apparel goods and will subsequently pay special attention to the procurement of raw materials and machinery through specialized agents. These discussions will clarify the manner in which the apparel firms produce their goods.

According to interviews, the flow of operations from production to sale can be depicted as in Fig. 4.1.

The important point is that some firms omit phase 2 of the process, and phases 3 and 4 often occur in reverse order. Some firms manufactured a limited quantity of a

Y. Iwasaki, *Industrial Organization in Iran*, SpringerBriefs in Economics,
DOI 10.1007/978-981-10-4579-0_4

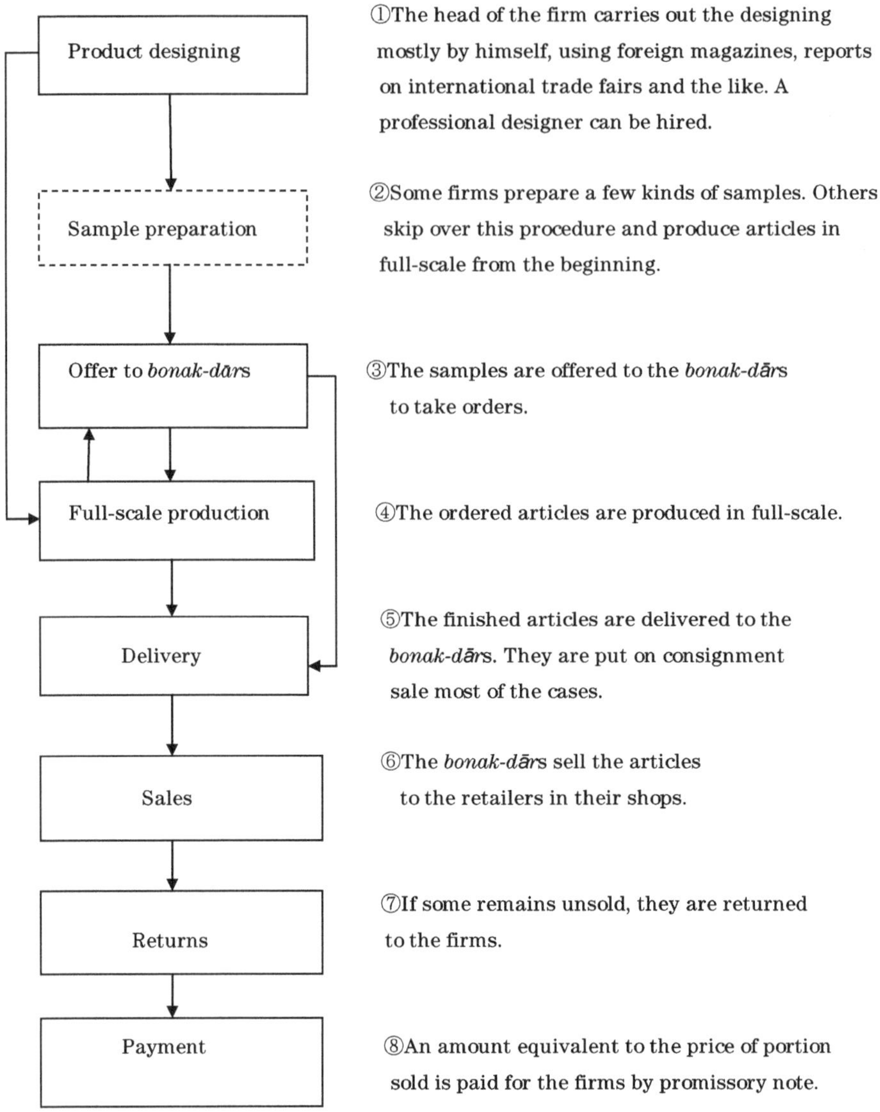

Fig. 4.1 Work flow from apparel production to wholesaling. *Source* Prepared by the author

certain model by way of an initial trial, gradually shifting to full-capacity production in keeping with regular costumers' feedback. Other firms produced a certain quantity of a certain model from the beginning and put all the products for sale on consignment.

The smaller a firm's scale, the more a firm was likely to employ the latter way of production. Of course, they could accept additional orders after the first production run.

In any of these cases, however, the contracted distributors never tended to specify product standards (such as design, color, and size). Distributors only selected some of a firm's designs and notified the firm of the quantity they would purchase.

A firm like Firm T, which was one of the informants in the 1998 interview survey (see Table 3.1), was involved in phase 4 in the process. Such specialized embroiderers customarily accepted extremely detailed directions along with raw materials from the ordering parties. But in a few cases, embroiderers were entrusted with designing the embroidery when the customers appreciated their capability.

4.2 Characteristics of the Production Process

Does the above-mentioned flow of operations from production to sale have anything to do with the organizational characteristics of apparel-producing firms discussed in the previous chapter?

To investigate this, a comparison with Japan, one of the biggest apparel-producing countries, is beneficial for determining the answer. Accordingly, a brief illustration of the Japanese industry will be presented next.

4.2.1 The Japanese Case

Conventionally, there have been many instances in Japan whereby firms, commonly called 'seizō-oroshi,' establish their own brand and expand their market throughout the country.

These firms are categorized as "apparel manufacturing wholesalers" (hereafter AMW) and their function can be summarized as follows: they plan, produce, and sell products at wholesale taking on risks themselves (Matsuo 1997, 49). In addition, "they don't necessarily operate their own factories" (Matsuo 1997, 49). Instead, they rely on either many petty sewing firms that accept part of the manufacturing processing or their lower tier subcontractors to carry out most of the actual production process. But the contract between AMWs and their contractors are in principle made under the condition that all the business risks are taken by AMWs.

Therefore, AMWs are responsible for procuring raw materials and adjusting the product quantity. AMWs do not undertake actual production but rather the planning and wholesale of apparel products (and sometimes contact retailers directly). They are specialized only in the collection and analysis of consumer information and product development, while they outsource all production processes to outside firms. In this way, they try to improve business efficiency and earn their profit.

We often find cases where a number of petty firms gather around AMWs in a certain place, known as an apparel-producing center in Japan. In such a case, a production system almost like a single body is formed through a division of labor and cooperation among agglomerated firms. This process occurs because firms of the same industry gathering in one place generate economies of scale in various aspects such as procurement of raw materials, information sharing, transportation, and division of production process.

In this context in Japan, the above-mentioned AMWs practically integrate and lead the production system in every producing center. That is to say, innumerable petty contractors are under the umbrella of an AMW that has the necessary planning capability and funds. Thus, apparel-producing centers have evolved in various districts.

Under these circumstances in Japan, (1) all phases in the production process are essentially outsourced since division of labor inside the producing center is common and firms with large business volumes play a role as AMWs, (2) the firm that takes the initiative in product planning is not the producing factory but the AMW who functions as distributor, and (3) most of the products are usually given directly to retailers, with few secondary wholesalers involved.

In contrast, the following can be identified as the characteristics of Iran's apparel-production system.

4.2.2 Firm Scale and Degree of Reliance on Outsourcing

Generally, apparel-producing firms are not very large no matter where in the world they are located. This can reflect the fact that apparel production is a comparatively easy skill to learn and requires a lower initial investment, thus making it manageable even for tiny investors to enter the market.

In Japan's case, firm scale and degree of reliance on outsourcing are generally in proportion to each other since larger firms take responsibility for such coordination. AMWs (or the substituted firms) coordinate the specialized factories in every phase of the production process; therefore, most parts of a product are in fact produced by outsourcing.

In Tehran, however, the circumstances are different. Larger firms that export and have established their own brand in the domestic market are more reluctant to outsource. They prefer carrying out all the processes in-house (from planning to finishing). Some even have their own weaving sections. In the 1998 interview survey, such firms discussed the problems arising in outsourcing: "there are fears that the model is copied," "it is difficult to control the quality in sewing process," "the products do not meet the order in standard," "the delivery of products is often delayed," and "monitoring cost is high." Many firms had concluded that outsourcing should be avoided as much as possible based on their own experiences.

In case of unexpected additional orders they might inevitably outsource. But Firm B remarked:

> We hardly outsource since the producer determines what to make and how much.[1]

This statement indicates that basically any firm does not produce based on orders. The fact they never make a production plan exceeding their own production capability results in the rarity of outsourcing.

As shown in Chap. 3, however, conditions are not the same as far as small-scale firms are concerned. Some informant firms in the 1998 interview survey were outsourcing all processes excluding sewing (Firm BJ and Firm R) or knitting (Firm FI and Firm N). On the whole, smaller firms relied more on outsourcing.

The important point here is that all the informant firms were carrying out product planning themselves and also remained responsible for procurement of raw materials and selection of contractors. In other words, these small-scale firms played a similar role to AMWs in Japan.

The important difference between these small-scale firms and the Japanese AMWs, however, was that the firms in Tehran were also involved in the actual production process. In addition, the production process assigned to the firm that took responsibility for coordination varied: Firm BJ was in charge of the sewing process, and Firm FI was in charge of knitting.

Another way that small-scale firms in Tehran differ from Japanese AMWs is that the firms who place orders resemble their contractors from the viewpoint of firm scale. This means that this kind of contract relationship is only found among small-scale firms gathered in Tehran, and they rarely come under a larger firm's umbrella. In a district where firms gather, a situation emerges wherein many petty firms stand side by side in multitenant buildings three or four stories high, a firm owner outsources his own work to the neighboring firms, and firms support each other through division of labor. Unlike the systematic business relationship between Japanese AMWs and their contractors, which run from upstream to downstream, Tehran-based firms tend to exhibit a "cooperative" work process by which a petty firm shares its production process with others and overcomes its capital weakness.

The reason why Iranian large-scale firms are reluctant to outsource can be summarized as follows:

First, labor costs are relatively low. Firm JG, a large-scale firm that holds all the production processes in-house, remarked:

> It is more profitable for the long term to give workers inside the firm certain training.[2]

For this reason, some firms outsource only the specific work stages done by machines, such as weaving or embroidery, while they do the handworks like finishing on their own.

Second, quality control is quite difficult. Many large-scale firms are apprehensive that their brand may be damaged in case of outsourcing.

---

[1]Interviewed on November 14, 1998.

[2]Interviewed on November 24, 1998.

> It is impossible for us to supervise the sewing process in detail in outside firms. [Firm JB][3]

> To avoid the information about design, color and materials being stolen, we must do everything in-house. [Firm G][4]

If any faults are found in outsourced products, the loss due to the recovery cost and damage to the brand will be serious in the long run. Every informant firm pointed out that outsourcing carries considerable risks.

On the contrary, few small-scale firms indicated the same concern.

> A certain pattern of embroidery, a certain sort of fabric…when a best-selling product comes up everyone follows it….the question is not the rightness in product planning but the state of market. [Firm B][5]

> We release a model in the market after making a backbreaking effort. Four or five customers no sooner come to buy them than we display the goods, and they copy them in an instant then sell 300 *tūmān* cheaper. [Firm D][6]

These remarks show that many small-scale firms are producing apparel goods that imitate the color and design of other firms' best-selling products. The copied products appear on the market at considerably low prices. While "copying" is usual, the problem of quality control is not seriously recognized. The situation seems to foster wide-scale outsourcing.

Based on the foregoing, the apparel-producing firms in Tehran can be divided into two groups. The first group contains certain large-scale firms that have a certain brand and rarely outsource due to a desire to protect their brand. They actively export and supply products at relatively high prices. The second group is made up of smaller scale firms (including some large-scale firms from the statistical point of view) that pay little regard to product quality and supply products only for the domestic market. The second group is an overwhelming majority among apparel firms. These observations suggest that in a sense, the apparel market in Tehran (and also Iran) is divided into two parts. Namely, the two groups target different customer strata in different markets, respectively.

4.2.3 Initiative in Product Planning

According to the interview surveys, each firm carries out product planning independently, regardless of the firm scale. Each firm decides what designs to implement, what material to use, and what quantity to produce. At a glance, this system seems extremely inefficient. This leads to the question: what factors or forces support its continued existence?

[3]Interviewed on November 19, 1998.

[4]Interviewed on November 24, 1998.

[5]Interviewed on November 14, 1998.

[6]Interviewed on November 21, 1998.

In general, it is natural that product planning is carried out by an economic actor who is supposed to have better information from the viewpoint of sales strategy, such as consumer preferences or market conditions, i.e., distributors. In Japan's case, AMWs, the de facto the distributors, play this role.

In Tehran, the persons in charge of specialized sections in large-scale firms are the ones who collect information, which firms use to plan their operations. They secure personnel in-house who have the same information as the distributors by paying a certain cost. In petty and small-scale firms who lack such a section, they may contact *bonak-dārs*—who are able to collect more consumer information—as input information to their product planning. But *bonak-dārs* are never involved in the planning phase in reality.

Some interesting remarks were made in the interview by interviewed firms. Firm R said:

> *Bonak-dārs* would never think of giving firms the information about color, size, and design in advance. If they do, they must certainly buy a large quantity of goods from that firm.[7]

The passivity of *bonak-dārs*' in product planning can be inferred from this remark, although they certainly seem to possess consumer information to some extent.

To the question about their method of product planning, most large-scale firms responded with "using a foreign fashion magazine for reference," "attending an international trade fair to get an idea," and "turning those ideas into a product to meet the Iranian's taste." As for small-scale firms, it is noteworthy that they remarked, "the Bazaar's product lineup should be helpful; we often imitate the products put on sale."

A majority of Iran's apparel-producing firms are small scale. In other words, most firms copy other firms' products and attach little importance to the customer information collected directly from the distributors, with a few exceptions of large-scale firms who develop an original model for the Iranian market.

Excessive admiration of existing brands also indicates the approach of apparel firms that dismiss the value of customer information.

> Name-brand products are strong seller in Iran. The consumers buy even shabby goods as long as they have the brand logo. [Firm D][8]

> Both in Tehran and in the provinces, people prefer brands. Even if the climate is different, they buy name-brand goods sent from Tehran. [Firm G][9]

Apart from the truth of "people's inclination to existing brands," it can be said at least that product planning based on advance market research has not yet become widespread.

In addition, it is important to focus on the state of Iran's apparel market. As stated before, the apparel market in Tehran (and also Iran) is divided into two parts,

---

[7]Interviewed on November 18, 1998.

[8]Interviewed on November 21, 1998.

[9]Interviewed on November 24, 1998.

and large-scale firms and small-scale firms target different customer strata in these respective markets. In the segments targeted by large-scale firms, firms produce goods in-house based on the information they gather directly. On the other hand, the market segments targeted by smaller firms—which form a large percentage of Iran's domestic market—have been described as follows:

> People do not pay attention [to factors] other than prices. They never care about the quality of fabric and sewing, or size. [Firm D][10]
>
> People first buy meat and bread. Clothes are next. [Firm FI][11]

In this market, as long as the product is cheap, added value is not particularly expected. At least the firms seem to think so.

One of the reasons why these firms eagerly copy other firms' products—other than differentiation from competitors—is that they realize that many consumers are concerned with the price more than the actual design. If *bonak-dārs*, who have more information about consumers' taste, take the initiative in product development, they might barely win the competition with small-scale firms who produce goods quite casually. Since in that case, *bonak-dārs* have to recover the cost of information-gathering first and then build up a certain large-scale production system to keep the unit price very low.

Moreover, the fact that the relation between producers and distributors is comparatively weak makes it more difficult for *bonak-dārs* to participate in product planning. *Bonak-dārs* are generally recognized to lack practical knowledge of apparel production:

> *Bonak-dārs* do not have any technical knowledge of apparel industry. Even a *bonak-dār* with 30 years' experience may not know about a kind of fabric. [Firm BJ][12]
>
> They are not specialists. [Firm JB][13]

Some firms also feel mistrust toward the *bonak-dārs* who are their business partners.

> I do not think using *bonak-dārs* is the best way. [Firm B][14]
>
> They never assume risks. All the risks in production are shouldered by apparel firms. [Firm BJ][15]
>
> The producer works hard to produce, and the retailer works hard to sell. But *bonak-dār* works in comfort. [Firm JG][16]

---

[10]Interviewed on November 21, 1998.
[11]Interviewed on November 25, 1998.
[12]Interviewed on November 14, 1998.
[13]Interviewed on November 19, 1998.
[14]Interviewed on November 14, 1998.
[15]Interviewed on November 14, 1998.
[16]Interviewed on November 24, 1998.

The apparel firms and *bonak-dārs* do not have mutual confidence since their activities are clearly differentiated and they know little about each other's profession. This differentiation makes it difficult for *bonak-dārs* to select the appropriate raw materials and partners if they desired to organize the production system.

4.3 Procurement System for Machinery and Raw Materials Through *Namāyande*

Now, we focus on the procurement system for machinery and raw materials that emerged after the 1979 Revolution under circumstance wherein even small-scale firms operated totally independently.

In Japan's case, strong AMWs are responsible for procuring raw materials and adjusting producing quantity. Contractors only receive the orders together with the raw materials that have already been prepared by AMWs.

Nevertheless, as we have seen, Iran's apparel industry lacks such production organizers. Therefore, each firm has to procure the necessary materials and even machinery by themselves.

As already mentioned in Chap. 2, the government established Centers for Procurement and Distribution to directly control imports after the 1979 Revolution. Imports of intermediate goods such as raw materials and machinery for the domestic manufacturing fell under complete government's control, and the Centers themselves purchased goods from suppliers abroad. The textile and apparel industry, which heavily relied on imported intermediate goods, was not an exception.

A majority of goods were distributed to domestic state-owned firms through the Centers. In parallel with this system, a way existed for private firms and factories with special permission (that is, foreign currency allocation) from the government to purchase foreign goods directly. Yet the distributors who wanted to import goods for sale were excluded as only the producers were allowed, in principle, to import the raw materials they needed.

In other words, even private small-scale firms had to participate in the import business, acquiring somehow permission from the government if they wanted to use foreign materials in production. Needless to say, the bureaucratic procedures for such permission were extremely troublesome.

This situation prevailed until changes were made to the Iranian government's trade policies in the early 2000s. Under such circumstances, small-scale firms that were unwilling to waste time and labor would utilize an agent called a *namāyande* to handle their imports (Iwasaki 1998, 2004).[17] A *namāyande* is an import agent who negotiates with foreign suppliers on behalf of apparel-producing firms who

[17]*Namāyande* is a Persian common noun meaning representative or agent. For example, members of Iran's national assembly are also called *namāyande*.

want to purchase raw materials and machinery from abroad. Rather than being local sales agents of foreign companies, as is usually the case, the *namāyande* would specialize in purchasing goods for local buyers.

They would search for a supplier in accordance with the buyer's (that is, the domestic apparel-producing firm) request, negotiate for an estimated price, and take a commission if the contract is successfully concluded. Such intermediation is the *namāyande*'s basic role.

Let us now examine how the procurement system worked in this period, that is, after the 1979 Revolution until quite recently, with the *namāyande* to help the innumerable small-scale firms operating independently.

4.3.1 1990s Field Survey on Namāyande

The author's research on *namāyande*'s role was conducted through periodic interviews and field trips, which were held in Tehran and its surrounding regions from 1994 to 1996. The *namāyande*'s business methods were examined mainly with the cooperation of Informant J, a *namāyande* residing in Tehran and who had been in business since the 1960s.[18]

The actual number of *namāyande* working with textile and apparel firms was not known. Even the registration bureau of Tehran Chamber of Commerce did not possess the number because when a *namāyande* registers, he reports only the corporate name; no details are recorded about the content of the business (interview with Informant R2, see Table 4.1). However, their number did not appear to be so great, a few hundred at most, in view of the average number of clients (200 or so) that a single *namāyande* could have [interviews with Informants J and A].

The author supplemented this on-site research with information from the Chamber of Commerce, Industries and Mines (otāq-e bāzargānī, sanāye'va ma'āden-e Tehrān), MAI, the Ministry of Commerce (vezārat-e bāzargānī-ye Īrān), the Ministry of Industries (vezārat-e sanāye'-e Īrān), and various organizations attached to these ministries, plus interviews with other *namāyande*; as well as visits to inspect factories in Tehran and the surrounding regions (see Table 4.1).

[18]Most of the research on the *namāyande*'s basic business methods was carried out at J's office and at his home. The author tried as much as possible to provide a picture of *namāyande* in general and not to note certain characteristics that seemed particular to the informant, and yet the description presented here should not be considered as applicable to all *namāyande* working with textile and apparel firms who are said to number several hundred.

Table 4.1 List of informants in interview surveys 1994–1996

Informant code	Specialty	Date of interview
J	*Namāyande* (involved in textiles)	Almost once a week during May 1994–Feb 1995, 26 Dec 1995, 5 Jan 1996, 14 and 19 Nov 1996
A	*Namāyande* (involved in textiles)	Every two to three months during May 1994–Feb 1995, Nov 14, 1996
S2	*Namāyande* (involved in machinery parts)	Nov 23, 1996
B2	A staff member in J's office	Jul 13 and Dec 9 1994
A2	Woolen fabric firm (employing 30 workers)	Oct 13, 1994
J3	Cotton fabric firm (employing 10 workers)	Oct 13, 1994
P	Marketing manager at a governmental textile company (employing 1700 workers)	Nov 18, 1996
AS	The Association of Iran Textile Industries	Nov 14 and 18 1996
R2	The Tehran Chamber of Commerce	Nov 20, 1994
M	Japanese trading company (textile marketing section)	May 26, 1994
Y	Japanese trading company (textile marketing section)	Jun 18, 1994
K	Japanese trading company (textile marketing section)	Dec 15, 1994

Source Prepared by the author

4.3.2 The Legal Standing of Namāyande

Intermediaries in Iran are legally divided into a number of categories. The *namāyande* fall under the category of intermediaries, known as *dallāl*. Iranian Commercial Law (qānūn-e tejārat) defines a *dallāl* as "a person who for a service fee intermediates the execution of business transactions or who finds customers for people wanting to transact business" (Article 335). A point to note is that when executing their intermediation, the *dallāl* himself, as a principle, does not deal in any goods. They do not bear the risks involved in the actual trading of goods, and the rights to the possession of goods are not transferred through the *dallāl*. Intermediaries who handle the buying and selling of goods as agents representing the actual parties in a transaction are legally differentiated from the *dallāl*.

Intermediaries classified by law as *dallāl* are divided by custom into two categories. One category is made up of middlemen known as *vāsete* or *dallāl*, who only intermediate in transactions between domestic firms. The other category is the *namāyande*, who intermediate in transactions with foreign companies. Thus in common usage, *dallāl* are associated with the former category (*vāsete*) and not latter, although legally both fall into the same category.

The *namāyande* themselves can be separated into two types: those who assist foreign suppliers in their sales activities in the domestic market,[19] and those who assist local buyers who want to purchase goods from abroad. We will examine the second type of *namāyande*, those who act as agents for local private firms and assist them in purchasing goods from abroad. Hereafter, everything concerning *namāyande* is to be understood as referring to this type and confined specifically to the textile and apparel industry.

Their names are registered with the Tehran Chamber of Commerce as *dallāl* or as trading companies, not as *namāyande*.[20] They cannot get approval to do business if they have a criminal record, they have to submit certain documents and meet particular requirements to set up an office, and *namāyande* are required to pay the chamber an annual membership fee.[21]

4.3.3 Namāyande's *Business Activities*

The principal role of the *namāyande* is that of an agent for private companies, mostly small-scale and medium-scale firms, who want to purchase machinery or materials such as threads, dyes, and fabrics from foreign companies. The *namāyande* conduct negotiations with the foreign companies in compliance with the demands of their domestic clients. There are *namāyande* functioning as intermediaries in every sector of the textile and apparel industry.

The *namāyande* regularly collect information on who wants to buy or sell how much of what product at what price. They provide this information to both buyers and sellers, carry out the negotiations, get pro-forma, then after the transactions have been completed, they receive from each party several percent of the transaction's value as a service fee.[22] A *namāyande* seems able to receive a fee from both parties even though he is the purchasing agent for the buyer is because most local firms buy foreign products only through their own particular *namāyande*, and this puts him in a position where he can demand a fee from the seller as well. Thus, when a foreign company tries to sell a product to a local firm, the latter will enter into a transaction only through the *namāyande* whom the firm owner recognizes as his agent. This means that the foreign company cannot sell its product directly to

[19]Interview with Informant K. This type of *namāyande* corresponds to ordinary sales agents found in other places. But in this period, Iran offered little possibility for them to work due to above-mentioned trade controls by the government.

[20]Interviews with Informants J and M.

[21]Interview with Informant R2, on November 20, 1994.

[22]The percentage varies depending on the kind of commodity imported and the method of delivery:1% for bulk purchases of standard commodities; 3% for large-size machinery that is difficult to transport; several percent more for products imported for experimental purposes; etc.

the local firm. There are a great number of small-scale firms in Iran's apparel industry that operate this way.[23]

These firms provide several reasons for choosing to work through *namāyande*.[24] One is the language problem; it is difficult to transact business directly with foreign companies. In addition, it is cheaper to deal through their *namāyande* than set up a section to handle imports within the firm. A third reason is that should trouble arise with a transaction, a company has its *namāyande* on hand to take care of any ensuing problems.

Beyond these reasons, firms also say that the long years of association with their *namāyande* guarantees a relationship of mutual trust when dealing with a foreign company with whom they can hardly expect to develop such a relationship. Thus, even if a foreign company has had a number of past dealings with a local firm, it will have to continue doing its business through the recognized *namāyande*, and for this reason, the *namāyande* can ask foreign companies for a service fee as well.

However, foreign companies can also find it useful to work through the *namāyande* because it saves them from having to contact numerous small-scale firms and collect a large number of small-lot orders. Furthermore, when undertaking comparatively large-lot transactions, foreign companies can gauge the reliability of customers who have few problems, such as collecting payments, if introduced by *namāyande*.[25]

4.3.4 Information Provided by the Namāyande

Besides their basic business as agents, when intermediating transactions, the *namāyande* also provide their clients (local buyers) with specific kinds of information. One kind is basic information on the products that clients want to buy, such as the prices, quality, and suppliers. Some of the most important information for small-scale private firms is where they can find the quantity of the goods they want to buy at how cheap a price, and the acquisition of such information depends on the skill and ability of their *namāyande*.

The *namāyande* also have to be up-to-date on technology and know about the latest developments in textile products and machinery. For this reason, they commonly specialize in areas such as production machinery or threads and fibers although it is usual for a single *namāyande* to specialize in several areas.

The *namāyande* also provide information on the current economy, such as size of the annual cotton harvest and current price of crude oil, which affects the size of the government foreign exchange reserves. They also provide information on revisions in government laws and regulations affecting the import business. The fact

[23]Interviews with Informants J and M.

[24]Interview with Informant J3, on October 13, 1994.

[25]Interview with Informant Y, on June 18, 1994.

that the *namāyande* keeps his clients informed about this sort of noneconomic information, especially in Iran where the regulations are very frequently revised,[26] can be a great help in softening its impact on small-scale firms.

Yet another important kind of information the *namāyande* can provide is technical understanding about business transactions. If a client asks about methods of payment, methods of transportation, or other such matters, the *namāyande* can provide the relevant know-how prior to the contract. For example, a company owner might says to his *namāyande*, "I would like to import this particular commodity, process it in my company, then export the product." The *namāyande* will then find out what regulations affect the importation of that commodity, what would be the cheapest way to transport it, suggest someone who might be good to work with in the venture, and introduce an export agent from among his own clientele.[27]

All of this information is provided to the client free of charge. Only after the transaction has been brought about does the *namāyande* collect a fixed portion of the value of the transaction from both parties as his service fee.

4.3.5 Namāyande's *Information Collection Methods*

Basic information on commodities, market prices, exchange rates, and the like can be obtained from business magazines, specialized journals, and other forms of domestic and foreign media. In addition, *namāyande* themselves or members of their office staff often travel abroad to collect information; if the *namāyande* is a large-scale operator, he can maintain overseas offices for collecting information and keeping track of product development, trends in raw material prices, what major foreign companies are doing, and other pertinent matters. However, *namāyande* business operations are normally not very large. A usual office will be headed by the *namāyande* with a few people working under him. Large-scale operations with a domestic office employing a dozen or more people and with permanent overseas offices staffed by Iranians are exceptions.

---

[26]A case in point are the 125 revisions to the laws and regulations concerning importing announced during 1373 (Iranian calendar, March 1994–March 1995). These revisions seem to affect importing directly and concern such matters as customs rates on different kinds of imported commodities,import–export treaties, and agreements with other countries in the region, central bank notifications, and the like. Among these revisions were nine regulations concerning the application of the import–export law. Besides these, an immense number of new regulations and notices were announced, practically on a daily basis. They can all be found in the official gazette, but their profuse number means that it is difficult to check all changes completely. Such official information is now being organized and categorized by private information research companies and provided to their customers (Markaz-e Ettelā'āt-e Fannī-ye Īrān 1994/95).

[27]The *namāyande*'s major clients are the textile and apparel firms, but sometimes also include export dealers who handle textile products. These are traders without experience in dealing with foreign companies (who can be textile manufacturers, trading companies, or their local distributors), and they entrust their intermediary needs to *namāyande*.

The *namāyande* are responsible for analyzing information from abroad. Being greatly dependent on imported thread, dyes, and machinery,[28] Iran's textile and apparel industry has a strong need to be well informed about developments in overseas businesses. The *namāyande* have long years of experience and accumulated information, and for this reason, many firms rely on their judgment.

Regarding the noneconomic information mentioned above, the *namāyande* rely on their connections with friends and acquaintances in the government administration to learn about new policies affecting the textile industry and how these are to be enforced. They also keep in regular contact with the Chamber of Commerce and other business organizations to collect relevant information. If a *namāyande* has graduated from a school of higher education, he could have connections with former schoolmates in the ministries and government offices. The longer a *namāyande*'s time in business and the better he is known in business circles, the more readily he can obtain information.

4.3.6 *The* Namāyande *and His Clients*

The greater part of the *namāyande*'s activities are taken up with information collecting, as stated above. But another activity that consumes considerable time is maintaining regular contact with clients. In order to keep his business running, a *namāyande* usually builds up a regular roster of clientele in his area of specialization through his capacity to provide information, and he is continually working to procure information about his own clients. Most of these regular clients have a personal acquaintanceship with the *namāyande*. They are old-school friends, former fellow soldiers, childhood friends, relatives, or people whom these friends and acquaintances have introduced. In most cases, these clients do their purchasing through a particular *namāyande* or several *namāyande* whom they have known for

---

[28]It is virtually impossible to use published data to measure in any accurate way the extent of the Iranian textile (therefore apparel) industry's dependence on imported materials. But even rough estimates indicate that for both 1993 and 1994, imported raw materials (e.g., natural and synthetic fibers, thread, chemical dyes) accounted for at least 35–36% of the annual value of inputs by the textile industry. However, it seems that this annual value of inputs includes the value of thread, fabrics, and other imported materials used in domestically produced intermediate inputs. It also seems that some materials included in these inputs do not in fact fall into the category of imports related to the textile industry. All of these uncertainties can affect the real figures. But in any case, it would seem that the above annual value is on the low side and that the real figure is larger. The situation is the same for machinery; there are no detailed data on the value of imports and inputs, and these figures cannot be calculated. However, most of the machinery in use, from the spinning stage through weaving, dyeing, and up to patterning, is made in Europe and Japan (Markaz-e Āmār-e Īrān 1996, p. 171, pp. 258–259; Markaz-e Āmār-e Īrān 1997, pp. 178–179, pp. 282–283). Participants at the Iranian government-sponsored seminar, "Investigation of problems in the textile industry" also pointed out the industry's overdependence on imported materials and machinery (Otāq-e Bāzargānī va Sanāye' va Ma'āden 1983).

years.[29] Besides these regular clients, there might also be some temporary clients who suddenly need the help of a *namāyande* due to changes in government import–export policies.

Generally speaking, one does not see a *namāyande*'s child taking over his father's clientele and becoming a *namāyande*. This is because the relationships between a *namāyande* with his clients have been built up individually over many years of personal acquaintance. Most often, when a *namāyande* retires, a long-serving staff member may take over some of the clients and set up his own *namāyande* business.[30]

Keeping in contact with clients, particularly with regular clients, plays an important role in building trusting relationships for both the *namāyande* and his clientele. From what the author observed, as noted earlier, most of the time these relationships are not formed on an organizational basis but a personal basis. The *namāyande* will phone clients once a month, and in the case of close clients, as often as once a week. He will visit his Tehran-based clients directly. For about thirty minutes, the two will chat over tea as the *namāyande* inquires how his client is faring and maybe even offers some advice if the client is having a problem with his business. The *namāyande* maintains the same sort of regular contact even with clients who do not expect at the moment to have any direct business with foreign companies. Clients also pay friendly visits to the *namāyande* for the sake of business relations and when they want the latest information about industry developments.

Through these types of regular contacts, the *namāyande* re-enforces his ties with his regular clients, and they in turn are important in helping him develop contacts with new clients. *Namāyande* can get information from the Chamber of Commerce about newly registered companies and firms and use this to build up connections with new clients. But by and large, they gain new clients through introductions from their old regular clientele. For this reason, calling on a client and "asking after his health" (*ahvāl-porsī*) is one of the important business activities undertaken by every *namāyande*.

From the above description, it can be seen that the primary element of a *namāyande*'s business activities involves collecting information and keeping up with his clients' current business affairs. How well a *namāyande* can carry on this important part of his business is determined greatly by his own individual ability. He needs to be proficient in foreign languages and have an extensive network of contacts for collecting information. Also important for gaining the long-standing personal trust of clients is a certain degree of social respectability, and here it is helpful if the *namāyande* is a devout Muslim or has a higher education. Other traits useful in strengthening *namāyande*—client ties is coming from the same home district and speaking the same local language. One *namāyande*, for example, who

[29]Interview with Informant A2, on October 13, 1994.

[30]Interviews with Informants J and B2.

came from Tabrīz and spoke Āzarī as his native language had a pool of clientele in which more than 70% also spoke Āzarī as their native language.[31] In such ways, the *namāyande* depend on their personal ties with the owners of local private firms, and undertake the purchase of foreign products and materials on the latter's behalf.

4.3.7 Namāyande's *Functions*

To sum up, *namāyande* perform three important functions. The first of these is the all-important and indispensable function of intermediating between local buyers and foreign suppliers. The *namāyande* works as an agent at the request of small-scale firms to find appropriate suppliers who can meet these firms' demands. This is their first and foremost function, without which no relationship between firm and *namāyande* could exist.

The second function is the *namāyande*'s role as a management consultant to small-scale private firms. He carries out this secondary function in the course of performing his first function. Even very small-scale firms with only a few workers, including the owner, are normally not contractors. Owners of these small firms operate in accordance with their own individual plans and policies. It is not unusual for even small-scale firms to conduct business regularly with foreign companies for the import of materials. For firm owners, the state of the global cotton market, current trends in the consumption of textile products, and other such information are important to help them decide what to produce.

But it is difficult to constantly collect this sort of information at the actual site of production. Considering the manpower, costs, and trained personnel needed to do so, it is not practical for each firm to collect such information individually. Beyond the actual collection, very often the ordinary firm owner does not have the ability to understand or analyze the procured information.

As stated earlier, the information that a *namāyande* provides also includes its analysis. He collects information from around the world on the products that his clients need, and he may even advise them on what products are worth buying. He can even offer advice on how to improve product quality and suggest what types and how many products to produce (although this sort of *namāyande* involvement in production is quite rare). *Namāyande* will also exchange information constantly with Bazaar merchants to find out about current trends in demand. These merchants might make such comments as "Nylon will not sell anymore this year," or "black shirts are in excess supply prior to '*Āshūrā*,"[32] or "cotton goods are in short supply." The *namāyande* can then advise his clients that they "should purchase a certain color of thread," or "should not produce this and that product for a time."

[31] Interviews with Informants J and A.

[32] In Iran, the time of '*Āshūrā*, which is a religious event of Shi'a Muslims, believers wear black clothes in mourning for the martyrdom of Hosein.

The *namāyande*'s suggestions are only for the very short term but nevertheless, his clients rely on them to guide their decision-making.

At the time of a commodity's actual importation, the *namāyande* carefully guides his client through the intricate process of payments and shipment technicalities, and in some cases, he will complete these complicated procedures on behalf of his client. This is another important service the *namāyande* provides as a management consultant.

The *namāyande*'s third important function is adjusting transactions to balance the needs of his clients with those of the foreign supplierss. Like the second function, this too is a secondary one. Many Iranian apparel firms depend on imports for part of their materials. These firms are always looking for the best quality at the cheapest price. The greater the number of foreign companies involved in transactions, the greater the choice of goods. At the same time, foreign companies trading in Iran are always seeking to boost their sales volumes. As the *namāyande* works to balance buyer demands with supplier marketing needs, there are times when he has to gauge how much of what should be bought by what firm from whom.

It should be noted that in business transactions, the *namāyande* is basically on the buyer's side. When balancing each side's requirements, the *namāyande* is working to prevent the suppliers from being monopolistic and oligopolistic and to secure the involvement of the greatest number of suppliers. To do this, he recommends the purchase of different products and materials to different buyers in a way that buyers do not concentrate on one product from one company, or he recommends that clients adjust the quantity of their production output.

This balancing of buyers' and suppliers' needs is based on the *namāyande*'s short-term perspective. He is not concerned about managing demand for the apparel industry as a whole. But in Iran's apparel-producing business where foreign suppliers provide a substantial portion of the needed materials, the *namāyande*'s adjustments of purchases and sales work to prevent fixed relationships emerging between buyers and suppliers, and this is advantageous in assuring a broad range of choices for the buyers.

As a result, this way of working through the *namāyande* provides the firms with a more efficient system for making purchases (i.e., having the largest possible number of suppliers to choose from) while for the *namāyande*, this third function of adjusting and balancing transactions assures the continuation of his own business opportunities.

4.4 Why Was *Namāyande* Needed?

In Iran's apparel-producing system, there is a noticeable absence of large-scale firms who take the initiative in market research, product development, and organization of smaller contractors to engage in the actual production. Iranian apparel-producing firm lack close contact with distributors; therefore, product planning is carried out based on their own market prospects. Each firm, regardless of scale, operates independently. It is noteworthy that small-scale firms, which comprise the greater proportion of apparel-producing institutions, operate in this way, although a certain level of "cooperation" among the firms can be observed.

Under such circumstances, the procurement of raw materials and machinery is a crucial but ponderous task for each firm. Particularly when the government had imposed quite strict import restrictions, even small firms with little capability to do so were obliged to conduct import transactions.

The *namāyande* system has served as a solution to this difficult situation encountered by small-scale firms. The fact that the *namāyande*'s primary activity is providing information to expedite market transactions explains the firms' most direct motive for employing such services; a *namāyande* as a person possesses the knowledge that the firms lack in terms of collecting and analyzing information. This specific ability makes the *namāyande* necessary for these firms.[33]

Business management based on personal relationships is another factor making the *namāyande* a necessary actor for firms. It is important to stress that firms seek to strengthen their external information channels outside by developing reliable relationships through extremely personal ties with their *namāyande* in order to survive in Iran's fluid business environment.

The majority of the Iranian apparel industry lacks vertical relationships between firms and contractors as well as horizontal integration among producers. Independent firm owners seemed to distrust groups composed of numerous unspecified members who they did not know directly, instead attaching great importance to personal relationships. This pattern of neither contracting nor associating with other firms is possibly in part due to the above-mentioned tendency towards distrust, which manifests in the firm owners' avoidance of involvement in collective operations.

The relationship between a *namāyande* and his clients, which is based entirely on their mutual personal ties, can likewise be seen as a manifestation of this distrust. Firms develop very close personal relationships to assure their business's safety rather than rely on public or societal systems. The *namāyande* also bases his own business on the relationship with each individual firm owner and never approaches his clients as a collective business organization under the name of "XX Company." Moreover, a *namāyande* does not automatically pass his clientele on to his son. This fact also shows that the *namāyande* serves a function that fundamentally differs from mere brokering entities like trading companies. In other words, the

[33]Iran's apparel industry in this period offered very limited channels for collecting information from overseas markets. Unlike in neighboring Turkey, Iran had little inflow of foreign information through foreign direct investment or the mass media. The relatively underdeveloped state of Iran's mass media and the insufficient inflow of foreign capital were caused by nearly two decades of political confusion and economic difficulties, along with the 1979 Revolution, the Iran–Iraq war, and the ensuing international isolation Iran experienced. At the same time, however, the *namāyande* have existed since well before the revolution, indicating that even during the Pahlavi period, when relatively close interactions occurred with international society, firms tended to rely on these specialists to collect information.

namāyande and his clients believe that developing a certain mutual trust will be difficult once the *namāyande* becomes a company-like collective body.

As has already been shown, the Iranian government's trade policies underwent radical change during the early 2000s. As a result, plentiful quantities of raw materials for apparel products entered the domestic market from overseas by merchants specializing in each item, and access to foreign raw materials improved drastically, even within Iran. Before long, the small-scale firms that used to rely on the *namāyande* to procure raw materials became able to obtain the materials needed from the domestic market themselves. Consequently, the need to procure raw materials through the *namāyande* system shrank considerably.

References

Iwasaki, Y. (1998). The Role of the *Namāyande* in Iran's Textile Industry. *The Developing Economies 36*(4), 440–458.

Iwasaki, Y. (2004). *Teheran Shōbai Ōrai:Iran Shōnin no Sekai (Doing Business in Tehran: The Customs and Spirit of Iranian Merchants)*. Institute of Developing Economies, Chiba.

Markaz-e Āmār-e Īrān. (1996). *Sāl-nāme-ye Āmārī-ye Keshvar 1373 (Iran Statistical Yearbook)*, Tehrān.

Markaz-e Āmār-e Īrān. (1997). *Sāl-nāme-ye Āmārī-ye Keshvar 1374 (Iran Statistical Yearbook)*, Tehrān.

Markaz-e Ettelā'āt-e Fannī-ye Īrān. (1994/95). *Sāderāt, Vāredāt, San'at va Keshāvarzī: Qavānīn, Moqarrarāt, Bakhshnāme-hā (Exports, imports, industry and agriculture: Laws, regulations, directives)*. Tehrān.

Matsuo, T. (1997). *Zukai Apareru Gyōkai Handobukku (Illustrative Handbook of the Apparel Business)*. Tōyōkeizai Shinpōsha, Tokyo.

Otāq-e Bāzargānī va Sanāye' va Ma'āden. (1983). *Vīzhe-nāme: Semīnār, Bar-rasī-ye Masā'el-e Sanāye'-e Nassājī (Special Issue: Seminar, Investigation of Problems in the Textile Industry)*. Tehrān.

Chapter 5
Distribution Network of *Bonak-dārs*

Abstract Several clusters of *bonak-dār*'s shops specializing in the wholesale trading of apparel products can be found in the south of Tehran city. *Bonak-dārs* accept apparel products temporarily from firms, put them on sale, determine the price in accordance with supply and demand, and see the products off if sold. In this sense, the real market participants are the producers and the retailers between whom the right of ownership of merchandize is transferred. The main role the *bonak-dār* plays is not to sell individual commodities as wholesale but to provide a "place" that brings sellers and buyers together, as if the *bonak-dār* were "an auctioneer" in the market. This is the function that responds to the extreme minuteness and anonymity of the apparel-producing firms.

Keywords *Bonak-dār*'s shops clusters · Vizitōr · Selection of merchandise · Price determination · Setting up of marketplace · Auctioneer

5.1 Retailers and Apparel-Producing Firms

The previous chapter examined the apparel-production system in Iran, focusing on the production processes utilized in independently operating firms as well as their procurement system for raw materials and machinery through *namāyande*. This chapter will pay special attention to the distribution system of finished products.

Product planning in the apparel industry is extremely important as it requires timely supply. In Japan, AMWs are directly linked with retailers, because it is rational for them to shorten the distance from consumers as much as possible to promptly collect extensive consumer information. Due to the recent development of mass merchandisers, it is pointed out that even the profit earned by local wholesalers is shrinking.

In contrast, in Tehran, few apparel-producing firms make contact directly with retailers, as seen in the previous chapters. Instead, many of them secure markets by using the *bonak-dār*. They rarely advertise their products through mass media.

Y. Iwasaki, *Industrial Organization in Iran*, SpringerBriefs in Economics,
DOI 10.1007/978-981-10-4579-0_5

Although some exceptional producers are found that became well-known brands by word-of-mouth information, they are hardly able to generate original "vogue".

> Tehran always leads a fashion, but it takes a year to reach the provinces. [Firm JG][1]

> I suppose the markets in Japan and South Korea move very quickly, maybe monthly. It is not like that here. [Firm B][2]

These remarks indicate that the market's speed in reflecting current fashion trends is relatively slow in Iran. Furthermore, mass merchandisers have not sufficiently grown in Iran—including Tehran—and therefore, the role of the *bonak-dār*, who bundles the demand of a number of small retailers, is still quite important.

One notable characteristic of the apparel-production system in Tehran is the rather weak relationship between the apparel-producing firms and distributors (*bonak-dār* and retailers). Since both apparel-producing firms and retailers are comparatively small in scale, firms seldom contact retailers directly. The wholesalers (the *bonak-dār*) intermediate between them. In fact, the pattern that emerges in this sector is one of a seemingly chaotic production site into which countless independent firms are crowding.

But if we observe the situation in detail, it becomes apparent that they manage to run routine operations by utilizing the support functions the *bonak-dār* system as well as the *namāyande* system provide to meet their needs and enable their survival. This chapter will focus on the *bonak-dārs*' sales network, which secures distribution channels for the products.[3]

To investigate the *bonak-dār*'s business, the author conducted two interview surveys in 1999 and 2001, respectively. The subjects of investigation were 12 apparel *bonak-dār* who were operating in Tehran city, two apparel retailers, two apparel-producing firms, Trade Union Production and Vendor Garment Tehran, Trade Union of Knitwear and Socks (Ettehādīye-ye Senf-e Kesh-bāf va Jūrāb), and the relevant organizations such as Industrial Management Organization (Sāzmān-e Modīrīyat-e San'atī) (see Table 5.1).

5.2 Clusters of *Bonak-dār* Shops

Some clusters of *bonak-dār* shops specializing in the wholesale trading of apparel products exist in the south of Tehran city (see Fig. 5.1). As already mentioned, apparel-producing firms are spread across Tehran, even though the southern part of Tehran city is their hub. In contrast, the *bonak-dārs*' shops tend to be located within specific clusters with few exceptions. This indicates that it is extremely important for the *bonak-dār* to set up a shop somewhere in these clusters while being located in a certain place is not necessarily an indispensable condition for the producing firms.

---

[1]Interviewed on November 24, 1998.

[2]Interviewed on November 14, 1998.

[3]Regarding the work of the *bonak-dār* and the shop clusters, see Iwasaki (2002) and (2004).

Table 5.1 List of *bonak-dār* informants and results of interview surveys 1999 and 2001

Bonak-dār's code	Location of shop	Business items	Number of suppliers	Form of transaction	Number of customers	Customers' specialty	Form of transaction
TI	Tehran Bazaar	Men's, women's, children's clothes and underwear	300	Basically buying on nonreturnable basis	?	Provincial wholesaler and retailer	Basically selling on nonreturnable basis
TY	Tehran Bazaar	Men's, women's, children's clothes and underwear	300–500	Commission sale	?	Provincial retailer	?
TG	Tehran Bazaar	Men's, women's, children's clothes and underwear	50–60	Basically commission sale	100–200	Provincial retailer	Basically selling on nonreturnable basis
MPG	Pāsāzh-e Homāyūn	Children's clothes	200–500	Basically buying on nonreturnable basis	50	Tehran and provincial retailer	Basically selling on nonreturnable basis
TT	Pāsāzh-e Homāyūn	Men's, and women's clothes	200	Commission sale in a month	50–100	Tehran and provincial retailer	Basically selling on nonreturnable basis
MK	Bāzār-e Kākh	Men's, and women's clothes	150	Basically commission sale	?	Tehran and provincial retailer	Selling on nonreturnable basis
N3	Pāsāzh-e Āksford	Children's clothes	100–200	Commission sale in a month	100–200	Provincial retailer	Selling on nonreturnable basis
NZ	Bahār St.	Children's clothes	400	Commission sale in a month	700	Tehran and provincial retailer	Selling on nonreturnable basis
BA	Bahār St.	Babies' clothes	40	Buying on nonreturnable basis	150	Tehran and provincial retailer	Commission sale in a week
PS	Sākhtemān-e Pelāskou	Men's clothes	100–	Commission sale	100–200	Tehran retailer	Selling on nonreturnable basis
TPBP	Sākhtemān-e Pelāskou	Men's clothes	?	Commission sale in a month	500	Tehran and provincial retailer	Selling on nonreturnable basis
TM	Pāsāzh-e Kompānī	Women's clothes	/	/	?	Provincial retailer	Selling on nonreturnable basis

Source Prepared by the author

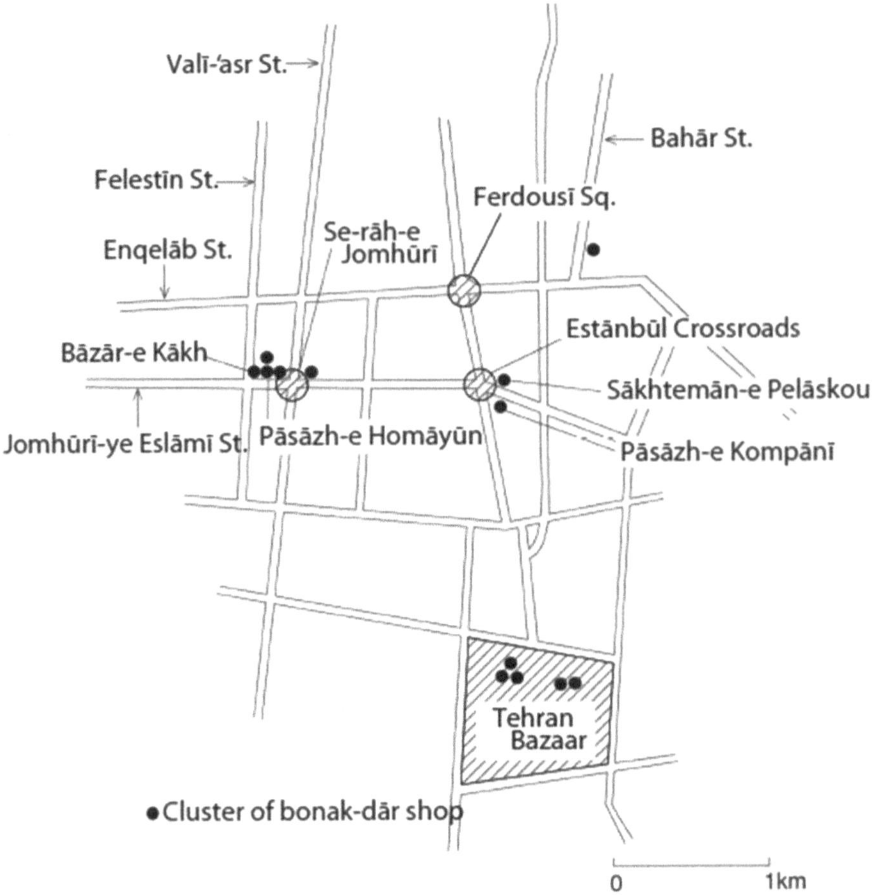

Fig. 5.1 Clusters of bonak-dar shops in Tehran. *Source* Prepared by the author

The clusters display a diverse range of sizes. Well-known locations for clusters are the Tehran Bazaar, with presumably thousands of apparel *bonak-dār* shops, Sākhtemān-e Pelāskou,[4] which is a big multi-tenant building with approximately 260 shops (as of 1999–2001), Jomhūrī-ye Eslāmī Street, along which several shopping arcades called *pāsāzh* are located with 30–100 shops, respectively. According to Trade Union Production and Vendor Garment Tehran, approximately 4000 apparel *bonak-dārs* were based in Tehran as of January 2011.[5]

These clusters are distinguished from one another based on the types of article in which they deal. For example, the clusters inside the Tehran Bazaar tend to trade

[4]Sākhtemān-e Pelāskou was collapsed by fire on January 19, 2017. I would like to extend my deepest condolences to the families and friends of the victims of the tragic incident.

[5]Interviewed on January 18, 2011.

in almost all apparel articles while the others specialize in specific articles such as "women's clothing only" and "children's clothing only."[6] Moreover, the price range differs in each cluster, even for the same article. The goods sold in the Tehran Bazaar are generally the cheapest and are accordingly of low quality, whereas those sold in other clusters are of better quality.[7]

The customers visiting these clusters are retailers from Tehran city as well as other provinces, in addition to provincial wholesalers. The main clientele also differs in each cluster. The customers of *bonak-dār*s located in the Tehran Bazaar are mostly provincial buyers, and many of them are "chance customers." As Table 5.1 shows, *bonak-dār*s normally do not record the accurate number of customers who buy goods from their shops, neither do they ask customers what kind of goods would be welcome to be collected for sale.

It is also noticeable that the relationship between *bonak-dār*s and apparel-producing firms is never static. *Bonak-dār*s are so-called "common agents" and do not specialize in wholesaling specific firms' products. Every *bonak-dār* is connected to a considerable number of suppliers (apparel-producing firms) since each firm only provides very small quantities of products.

All these features reflect the fact that Tehran is one of the biggest production centers of apparel products in Iran and at the same time is the biggest wholesale center. In most cases, products made in the provinces are initially sent to Tehran, from where they are dispatched again to local markets. This means that the clusters of *bonak-dār* shops in Tehran function as a major trading center of apparel products with links all over the country.

5.3 Collection and Sales of Apparel Products by *Bonak-dār*

The path that products follow through the distribution channel is as follows. As mentioned earlier, the apparel-producing firm takes the lead in designing the product. The information concerning buyers that the *bonak-dār* possesses—for example, his judgment on what kind of article attracts the retailer—is never shared with the firm.

---

[6]At the time of these surveys, Sākhtemān-e Pelāskou was famous for men's and boys' clothing, but few women's articles were found. Bahār Street was known as wholesale center of children's clothing especially newborns. Informant FK, a retailer, remarks "I visit Sākhtemān-e Pelāskou, or Jomhūrī-ye Eslāmī Street to buy men's and women's clothing. As for kids wear, I will find something in the upper (northern) part from Jomhūrī. Every district has own specialty." (Interviewed on July 5, 1999).

[7]According to the survey that the author conducted in August and September in 2001, variations in price range (therefore differences in product quality) among the clusters were clearly observed. The price of a men's autumn shirt was 30–50 thousand Rial in Tehran Bazaar, 52–75 thousand Rial in Sākhtemān-e Pelāskou, and 50–70 thousand Rial in Pāsāzh-e Homāyūn respectively. (Iwasaki 2002, 23–24).

Therefore, in most cases, the products (or samples) are brought into the *bonak-dār*'s shop by the apparel-producing firm. A person called a *vizitōr* is hired to promote the products. As the producing firms are generally very small and even the owner himself is engaged in the production activity, they have little time to visit *bonak-dārs* and take orders. Instead, the firm employs a *vizitōr* to visit *bonak-dārs*' shops, accompanied by the products (or samples) as a deputy sales staff.

In general, the single producing firm can hire several *vizitōrs* so that more *bonak-dārs* could be visited. The *vizitōr* also goes around collecting the apparel products from several producing firms, which are then shown together to *bonak-dārs*. Hence, the relations between firms and *vizitōrs* are not necessarily exclusive. The two parties can maintain their business relations for a while, but this is quite fluid in most cases. Even though a *vizitōr* is a very good salesman, a firm cannot monopolize him, and he remains as one of their business acquaintances. This seems to be a way for both *bonak-dārs* and *vizitōrs* to minimize their risk in case one of them is not good at making profit. When a contract with the *bonak-dār* is concluded, the *vizitōr* takes a percentage.

Some exceptional *bonak-dārs* do exist who collect products directly by visiting firms or trade fairs. However, the *bonak-dār* commonly only examines finished products or the samples that are brought in and selects articles that he considers as possible best sellers, after which he places his orders.

At the time of delivery, most *bonak-dārs* conclude contracts of commission sale with the firms (*amānat*), which are usually settled several months later. If any of the products remain unsold during the period, they are returned.

The *bonak-dār* does not engage in any particular sales promotion activity. He displays the collected products in his shop, and if he reaches an agreement with a retailer or with a provincial wholesaler who visits the shop, he signs up. Most *bonak-dārs* remarked in the interview that as a matter of principle, they never accept returns from the retailer or provincial wholesaler. In other words, the business is on a nonreturnable basis.[8] In cases where the customer is a provincial buyer, the *bonak-dār* undertakes dispatching the products.

If the goods consigned for sale remain unsold, they are returned to the producing firm. Then the amount due after deducting returns is paid to the firm in the form of a promissory note that falls due in a few months' time.

The above-mentioned process that the products undergo through the distribution channel indicates that the result of the interview surveys to *bonak-dārs* in 1999 and 2001 do not contradict the results of survey of producing firms in 1998. Quite a contrast however, emerged in that many *bonak-dārs* responded they rarely return products to the firms while the firms complained about perpetual risk of returns.

[8]In case that the product has a fault, or an alternative sales channel exists for the unsold product and the customer (the retailer) is close to the *bonak-dār*, they may accept returns. The *bonak-dār* BA in Table 5.1 exceptionally sells goods on commission for a week to retailers. It is plausibly because BA has its own production section in-house and attaches great importance to having steady customers for sales promotion of its own products.

Therefore, the principal activities of the *bonak-dār*s are maintaining a shop in a famous cluster, keeping the shop tidy, and displaying goods in an enticing way. Examples of *bonak-dārs* exceeding these tasks and engaging in the promotion of the items they sell are extremely rare.

That said, although the *bonak-dārs* are not directly involved in producing the items they sell, they carry out certain basic screening procedures as regards the products that the firms have supplied and judge which are likely to be best sellers. In other words, the *bonak-dār*s provide backing for sales in the cluster by grouping together various attractive items that they think will meet the customers' needs and that are within a reasonable price range. The wholesale price is determined by each *bonak-dār* after this screening step, with a profit being added to the producing firm's offered price. In this manner, some degree of competitive price adjustment occurs in every cluster.

5.4 Function of the *Bonak-dār*

As stated above, the *bonak-dār*s' basic function can be understood as collecting products from numerous apparel-producing firms scattered in various locations in Tehran (a major production center), displaying those with standard prices, and offering items to customers (the customers being retailers and provincial wholesalers).

Many producing firms grumble that the *bonak-dār*s never assume any risk concerning production. In fact, the majority of firms enter into contracts with the *bonak-dār*s for commission-based sales and are mindful of the fact that the *bonak-dārs* hold overwhelming sales power in the domestic market (Fig. 5.2 illustrates the above-mentioned relationships among the production and distribution systems). Here, we seek to identify some of the prominent roles the *bonak-dār*s play that are difficult for the producing firms and retailers to undertake, based on the interviews and the site observations by the author.

5.4.1 Setting up and Management of the Marketplace

The first point to consider is that the clusters of *bonak-dār*'s shops function as the central market of apparel products and ameliorate the distribution difficulties caused by of the miniscule scale of individual producing firms.

As shown in the previous chapters, the apparel-producing firms scattered across Tehran city mostly operate independently despite being small in scale. Moreover, few large-scale producing firms or leading distributors exist, who bundle such small producers. This distortion makes the situation difficult for both suppliers and buyers. That is, the small-scale producing firms are not able to secure markets through sales promotion activities because of their minuteness while retailers

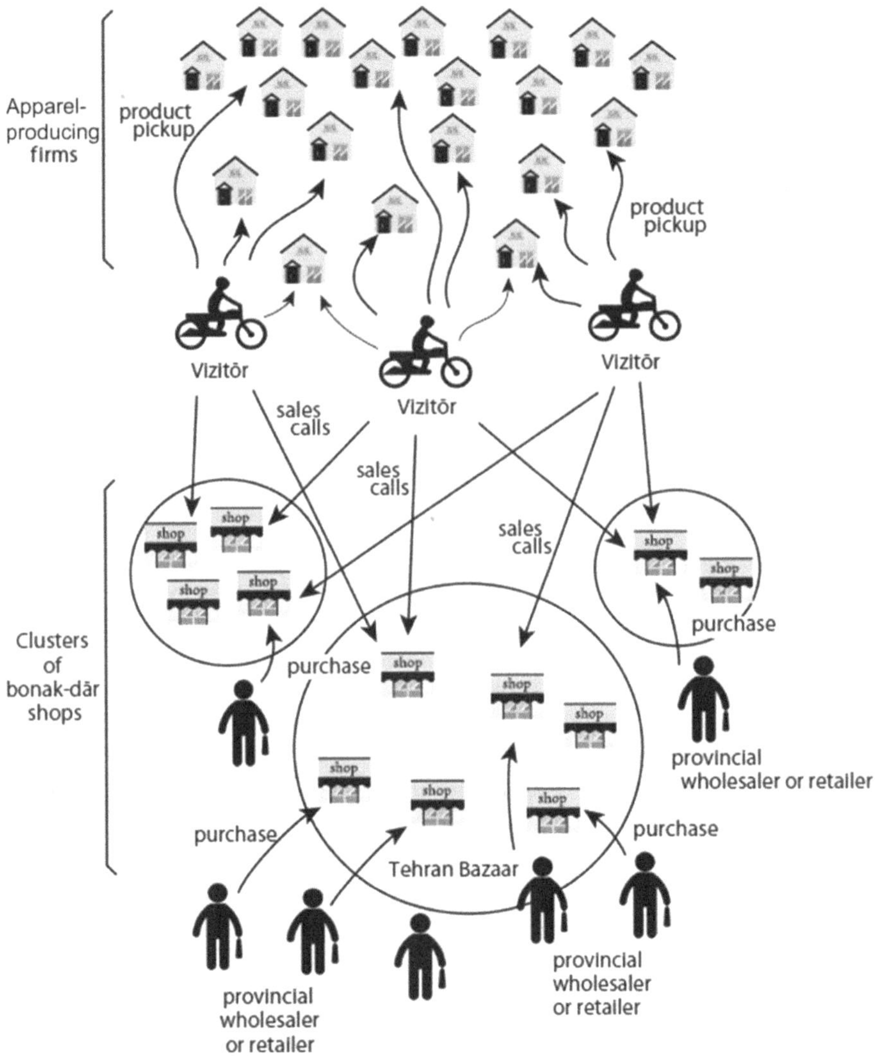

Fig. 5.2 Production and distribution of apparel products. *Source* Prepared by the author

seeking apparel goods are not well informed about where to buy them in the massive production center of Tehran. In other words, the countless apparel-producing firms operating in Tehran city are an extremely anonymous crowd for buyers.

Under such circumstances, the clusters of *bonak-dār*'s shops help suppliers in releasing goods and buyers in searching for goods; hence, they reduce the distribution difficulties to an extent.

Now, let us observe what risk the *bonak-dār* assumes in carrying out this wholesale function.

The majority of the *bonak-dār*'s expenses in the apparel goods wholesale market concern the cost of setting up a shop in an existing cluster. Some *bonak-dār*s possess the ownership or the usufructuary right (*sar-qoflī*)[9] of a shop while others merely rent a shop for their business. Sākhtemān-e Pelāskou, one of the *bonak-dār* clusters, was an individual's property. After the 1979 revolution, it was requisitioned and came under the supervision of the governmental foundation. In Tehran Bazaar, there are two types of shop occupations. One is the *mouqūfe* (religiously contributed property) shop, which can never be a subject of private possession or purchase, but its usufructuary right can be dealt with. The other type of shop can be bought and sold as ordinary real estate between individuals.[10] In all clusters, the cost of setting up shop is considerably high.[11] The *bonak-dār* becomes able to sell goods utilizing the drawing power of the cluster only after securing the place, which comes at a high price.[12]

Besides these initial high set up costs, *bonak-dār*s also bear the secondary expenses such as inventory management costs. While the apparel products are in the *bonak-dār*'s possession, he undertakes responsibility for maintaining the goods' quality. If the goods remain unsold, he sends them back to the producers. He also optimizes the volume of inventory by transmitting goods with poor demand to other *bonak-dār*s or lower stratum clusters.[13]

The *bonak-dār* bears the aforesaid cost of setting up and administrating the wholesale market, and as a result, the collection and sales of apparel products are extremely well facilitated in Tehran. The producing firms rely utterly on the *bonak-dār*s for sales promotion activities; therefore, they certainly benefit from the existence of the *bonak-dār* clusters.

It is incorrect to think that the *bonak-dār* never shoulders any risk in sales as the producing firms claim (see 5.5), even though he never purchases the apparel

[9]*Sar-qoflī* is generally known as a usufructuary right for commercial buildings in today's Iran. Regarding the historical circumstances under which *sar-qoflī* was established as a right and the actual state of its application and significance for trade, see Iwasaki (2011) and Iwasaki (2016).

[10]According to the author's investigation, there are more buildings in Tehran Bazaar that can be the subject of an ordinary transaction than *mouqūfe*.

[11]As of May 2001, the average monthly rent for a medium-sized shop is 4–4.5 million Rial in Pāsāzh-e Homāyūn, and 3.5–4 million Rial in Bāzār-e Kākh, respectively. The price of *sar-qflī* is about 1 billion Rial in Bāzār-e Kaffāsh-hā (the prime location in Tehran Bazaar) and 330 million Rial in another street in Tehran Bazaar. One US dollar is approximately equivalent to 8000 Rial. (Iwasaki 2002, 16).

[12]According to Industrial Management Organization, the average wages for a public employee in Iran is about 1.3 million Rial per month at the time of August 2001. As for a worker in private sector, it is about 1.075 million Rial (Iwasaki 2002, 25).

[13]The marketplace for unsold goods is generally called *bāzār-e estok* (dumping field). Informant PS pointed out Pāsāzh-e Āksford as an example. Goods are sent to such marketplaces, however, only when they are expected to remain unsold even in the next season (Iwasaki 2002, 25).

products outright from the producers. Informant MPG remarked that he had to close one of the shops he operated in the past. Other *bonak-dārs* have been driven to downsize or quit the business due to economic depression or their own mismanagement or poor judgment in selecting goods.

5.4.2 Selection of Merchandise and Price Determination

Another important point bearing consideration is that the *bonak-dār* clusters in Tehran are commonly recognized as *būrs* for respective articles among the people concerned. The term *būrs* originally meant "a stock exchange" and was borrowed from French. In contemporary Iran, another meaning has evolved—the place where information about an article is concentrated and therefore there the price of the article is determined. It suggests the possibility that the wholesale and retail prices for the provinces are determined on the basis of the wholesale price in Tehran's *bonak-dār* clusters.

The *bonak-dār* clusters can function as *būrs* despite not being direct suppliers of goods because each original seller (producing firm) has little control over the market. The sales channel is almost entirely limited to the *bonak-dār* clusters, and only the *bonak-dār*s are able to estimate the supply–demand balance across the whole market.

The *bonak-dār*, who specializes in the collection and wholesale of apparel products, reflects the Iranian circumstances in which neither large-scale producing firms nor any retailers undertake this task. Some producing firms have tried to open up the sales channels to others than the *bonak-dār,* but doing so poses a formidable challenge. Firm JB, a relatively large-scale producer, remarked:

> We opened our own shop, but closed it a year later. One shop in Tehran is not enough, we must have had more. But the place for retailing is very expensive and we were not known....[14]

Retailers who visit the clusters commonly recognize that each cluster operates at a certain price range. They expect the cluster that they visit to offer a wide assortment of items but within a certain price range. The *bonak-dār*s, as a matter of fact, do not accept all articles that producers offer but carefully screen them to eliminate products that are not best-selling as well as ones that do not fit the cluster's reputation. In other words, the *bonak-dār*'s screening, which is based on the customers' expectation, maintains the drawing power of the cluster, guaranteeing its sales volume.

After carrying out this screening process and bringing the products into the *bonak-dār*'s shop, the wholesale price is determined by each *bonak-dār* by adding

[14]Interviewed on November 19, 1998.

some profit to the producer price. No collusion in prices was observed among the *bonak-dārs* in a cluster. Informant TG, a *bonak-dār* in Tehran Bazaar said:

> I have no contact with other *bonak-dārs*. The producers supply goods to us and to others as well. It is impossible for the others to sell cheaper, since we stand such heavy cost for shop maintenance like water, electricity, tax... The others are also obliged to sell the same price.[15]

It is thus plausible that the wholesale price is determined quite competitively.

This method of segregation between the *bonak-dār* clusters results in buyers' convenience, and therefore, the drawing power of the clusters increases.

5.5 *Bonak-dār* as an Auctioneer

The *bonak-dār* in Tehran play many roles, as we have seen, and the following two can be considered the most important: (1) opening the wholesale market and (2) price determination. The *bonak-dārs* operating in each cluster appear to function as "an auctioneer" in the market, given the importance of the *bonak-dār*'s function in announcing a standard price for other markets across the country, whereas they never run a risk in terms of sales of any one individual commodity.

"An auctioneer" is a symbolic translation of the equilibrium price mechanism in the perfect competitive market. An auctioneer opens the auction, intermediates between a number of sellers and buyers who gather there, and induces the emergence of an equilibrium price. He is expected to never pursue his own profits in the auction but determine an appropriate price based on the balance between supply and demand.

It goes without saying that the actual *bonak-dār* can never be considered such a paragon of fairness and impartiality. The *bonak-dār* clusters are neither perfectly competitive markets nor even public markets open to anyone. Rather, the *bonak-dār* clusters are private markets held by the group of *bonak-dārs* itself.

The *bonak-dārs* accept the apparel products temporarily from the producing firms, put them on sale, determine the price in accordance with the supply and demand situation and see the products off if sold. In this sense, the real participators in the market are the producing firms and the retailers between whom the right of ownership of the merchandise is transferred.

There is, of course, an incentive for the *bonak-dār* to increase the overall trade volume because he gains more by doing so. But this incentive works more toward increasing the drawing power and the entire trade volume rather than by selling any individual commodity. The *bonak-dār* is not the real party concerned with each transaction but instead acts as an auctioneer so that a certain volume of transactions are closed.

On the other hand, the producing firms complain that the *bonak-dārs* do not assume reasonable risk. For example, Firm G interviewed in 1998 grumbled:

---

[15]Interviewed on July 5, 1999.

> The *bonak-dār* examines our products and take them away…if not sold, if the market doesn't response, if recession hits…what do they do, they return the products in the end. Then we become miserable.[16]

The fact that the *bonak-dār* assumes a part of sales risk through the cost of market maintenance may not very obvious for the producing firms. In view of the *bonak-dār*'s function in terms of the distribution process and the appended cost, however, the producers' criticism of the *bonak-dār* should not be indiscriminately upheld.

No discernible change in the *bonak-dārs*' functions were apparent even after 2000. Meanwhile, the conventional segregation between the clusters continues as before. Interestingly enough, in the 2008–2011 round of interviews with the relatively large-scale apparel-producing firms, some firms (such as informant firms H, KTI, and FZ) remarked that they have established sales channels without *bonak-dārs* as they found transactions with *bonak-dārs* problematic due to drawbacks such as the long terms of clearance and the risks of nonpayment. Others continued to recognize the value of the *bonak-dārs*, and one (Firm N2) remarked:

> It will not pay without *bonak-dārs*.[17]

It can be concluded that the main role that the *bonak-dār* play in the distribution of apparel products in Tehran is not to wholesale individual commodities but to provide a "place" that brings sellers and buyers together, a function that responds to the above-mentioned extreme minuteness and anonymity of Tehran's apparel-producing firms. The *bonak-dārs*' distributing function allows the independent apparel-producing firms to operate despite selling products at very low volumes. Without the agency of the *bonak-dārs*, the producers would be hard put to open up their own sales channels and maintain them on a day-to-day basis.

References

Iwasaki, Y. (2002). Teheran no Apareru Oroshiuri Shijō: Bonakudāru no Serinin Kinō (The *Bonak-dār* as Auctioneer: A Case Study of Apparel Wholesale Market in Tehran). *Ajia Keizai (Asian Economy) 43*(2), 2–25.

Iwasaki, Y. (2004). *Teheran Shōbai Ōrai: Iran Shōnin no Sekai (Doing Business in Tehran: The Customs and Spirit of Iranian Merchants)*. Chiba: Institute of Developing Economies.

Iwasaki, Y. (2011). *Sar-qoflī* in the Customs and Laws of Modern Iran: The Emergence of *Haqq-e Kasb o Pīshe o Tejārat* and the Evolution of the Shop-lease Contract System. *Iranian Studies, 44*(2), 147–174.

Iwasaki, Y. (2016). 'Shop-lease Contract with *Sar-qofli*' in the Post-Iranian Revolution Era: Deletion of '*Haqq-e kasb o pisheh o tejārat*' from the Law of Lessor-Lessee Relationships. *Iranian Studies, 49*(3), 359–381.

[16]Interviewed on November 24, 1998.

[17]Interviewed on January 30, 2011.

Chapter 6
The Apparel-Producing Center After Import Liberalization

Abstract Many wholesale shops that specialized in foreign apparel (mainly Chinese) had emerged in late 2000s in Tehran. Traders who engaged in bringing Chinese goods include the *bonak-dār*s, Tehran Bazaar apprentices who invested money in purchasing Chinese goods in partnership with others, and ex-producers who used to run apparel firms. Surprisingly, those who engaged in the import business after deregulation were not the established merchants under the existing distribution system but rather "newcomers" to the field. In particular, those who are involved in production activities demonstrate a high mobility between various business fields. Such an elastic relationship between the production and distribution functions as a safety valve for each firm under Iran's weakly organized system, where no vertical and horizontal relationships exist among firms. The Chinese system remarkably resembles the prototype forms of market trading, which may indicate a high affinity for the needs of firms operating under the Iran's weakly organized system, where there are no formal barriers to entry.

Keywords Wholesale clusters specializing in foreign products • Inflow channel • Guangzhou and Yiwu • Specialized Markets (zhuanye shichang) in China • Weakly organized system

6.1 The Age of Import Liberalization

As discussed in previous chapters, the main driving force of apparel production in Iran was originally provided by an agglomeration of small-scale firms, each employing fewer than 10 workers.

The industry's minute scale of operations is clearly shown by the fact that 98% of these firms were small-scale, employing fewer than 10 workers as of the mid-1990s (Markaz-e Āmār-e Īrān 1998, 200). Thereafter, the number of apparel-producing firms peaked at approximately 58,000, equivalent to 13% of all Iranian manufacturing firms in 2002/03 (1381). Again, nearly 99% of these firms were also small-scale firms with fewer than 10 workers (Markaz-e Āmār-e Īrān 2004, 259).

Y. Iwasaki, *Industrial Organization in Iran*, SpringerBriefs in Economics,
DOI 10.1007/978-981-10-4579-0_6

Regarding the apparel industry's contribution to Iran's manufacturing output, its share decreased throughout the above period. However, small-scale firms still accounted for 80% of the output (Markaz-e Āmār-e Īrān 2004, 273). Thus, as mentioned previously, the minuteness of firms is a distinctive feature of Iran's apparel industry.

According to available annual statistical data for the industry, albeit only for apparel-producing firms with more than 10 workers, it is evident that these large-scale firms (with more than 10 workers) were barely able to maintain production levels during the 12 years from 1997/98 (1376) to 2011/12 (1390) while the number of firms and workers underwent a considerable decline (see Tables 2.2, 2.3). We should, of course, remember that small-scale firms employing fewer than 10 workers (the majority of firms in the sector) do not appear in the official data.

Taken together, it should be pointed out that between 1997 and 2011, Iran's apparel industry showed the following traits: (1) The majority of the workforce worked in small-scale firms and (2) Large-scale firms with more than 10 workers—firms that are in the minority—maintained production levels despite many difficulties.

Meanwhile, after 2003/04 (1382), a rapid increase in apparel imports occurred. During the 1990s, the volume of apparel imports into Iran was negligible. In fact, the volume of imports increased approx. 11-fold between 2002/03 (1381) and 2003/04 (1382). Although the volume of imports dropped considerably in 2006/07 (1385), it again increased in 2008/09 (1387). Overall, the data show that compared to the preceding period, a substantially larger quantity of foreign-made apparel products flowed into Iran in a sustained manner after 2003/04 (1382).

The trend can be understood by taking into account Iran's general economic policies at that time (overviewed in Chap. 2). Let us now examine it in detail.

After the 1979 Revolution, the Iranian government introduced a regime of strict import controls that were intended to stabilize the exchange rate and allocate the distribution of commodities during the Iran–Iraq War. After the ceasefire, however, controls were maintained almost without change. While imports of intermediate goods were placed under centralized government control, meaning that only specified organizations, enterprises, and individuals were allowed to purchase them, imports of final consumer goods were prohibited. This prohibition of consumer goods imports carried the effect of blocking the inflow of undesirable Western cultural elements during the period immediately following the Revolution. The more substantial aim of this prohibition, however, was to regulate the exchange rate and protect domestic industries.

The import controls during this period were essentially enforced by combining several policies, including foreign currency allocation, the imposition of a licensing system on imports set by the Ministry of Commerce and the Ministry of Industries, and imposition of high tariffs [combining basic tariffs (hoqūq-e pāye) with commercial profit taxes (sūd-e bāzargānī)].

These centralized economic policies were gradually relaxed after the early 1990s owing to deregulation, a trend that rapidly gathered pace under the Khātamī government. This "liberalization" trend, typified by developments such as the privatization of state-owned enterprises was extended to encompass the government's trade policies and occurred simultaneously with the government's ballooning income due to a gradual rise in the crude oil price. This paved the way for a substantial easing of restrictions on imports. Although no explicit announcement of a change to the apparel import policy seems to have been made, after 2001/02 (1380), conditions applying to apparel imports were removed and the tariff rate, which had been over 200%, was dramatically reduced to 90%. The rate was lowered again to 50% in 2004/05 (1383), and after 2006/07 (1385), it was kept at the 100% level (Directorate-General for Export-Import Regulations 2004, 2005, 2006, Edāre-ye Koll-e Moqarrarāt-e Sāderāt o Vāredāt-e Vezārat-e Bāzarganī 2000, 2003, 2004, 2005, Trade Promotion Organization of Iran, Directorate-General for Export-Import Regulations 2008, Sāzmān-e Touse'e-ye Tejārat-e Īrān, Edāre-ye Koll-e Moqarrarāt-e Sāderāt o Vāredāt 2011).[1]

As a result of this deregulation, a substantial amount of foreign-made—mainly Chinese—apparel goods flowed into Iran in that period, a phenomenon reflected in the official statistics.

6.2 Emergence of Wholesale Clusters Specializing in Foreign Apparel Products

Fieldwork conducted by the author provides evidence for the substantial surge in foreign apparel imports that flowed into Iran. In late 2000s, Tehran saw the emergence of many wholesale shops specializing in foreign apparel products, something not seen in the 1990s. It would appear that "overwhelming the Iranian market with foreign apparel products" mentioned at the start of this volume has indeed come to pass (Iwasaki 2012b).

This chapter will discuss the ways in which foreign apparel products are distributed based on the results of interview surveys. The interviews were carried out at periodic intervals in Tehran during the years 2008–2011, with the respondents being apparel-producing firms and related traders (see Table 3.2).

6.2.1 Clusters of Wholesale Shops Trading in Foreign Apparel Products

Wholesale shops in Iran's contemporary apparel market specializing in foreign apparel products tend to feature one of two types of "foreign products." Some products are sold in high-grade shops operating inside the city as sales outlets for

[1]We should, however, note that if Iran's foreign exchange reserves were to deteriorate sharply in the future, import restrictions may be tightened again.

famous foreign brands[2]; the other products are those sold at extremely low prices in the conventional *bonak-dār* shop clusters (and surrounding areas). It goes without saying that in terms of the volume of goods sold, the latter category surpasses the former. The latter category, dominated by Chinese-made goods, first became an area of controversy in about 2004.

The best-known places in Tehran for the sale of cheap foreign apparel products are located in the Tehran Bazaar.[3] In areas such as Bāzār-e Soltānī, and Bāzār-e Mesgar-hā, many shops stand side by side where cheap and poor-quality apparel goods from China, India, and Thailand are displayed in a cramped manner. These products include women's clothing, underwear, children's garments, and the like. These clusters did not emerge immediately after the inflow of foreign apparel products. Rather, the traders who originally operated there dealt with cheap Iranian products, but they rushed, avalanche-like, into selling cheaper foreign goods after the early 2000s and their presence led to the formation of major clusters.

6.2.2 Inflow Channels and Sales Networks

Some interesting and surprising information emerged as a result of the interview surveys concerning the large amount of products being brought into the Iranian market and sold through local sales networks. Consider the following example.

First, it is evident that those who bring massive amounts of foreign apparel products (mainly Chinese goods) into the domestic market are mostly Iranian traders, quite a number of whom were formerly engaged in domestic apparel production in Iran.

According to interviews with apparel wholesalers in clusters located in the Tehran Bazaar as well as other sites across Tehran, three types of traders are engaged in bringing Chinese goods into Iran: (1) those who have been operating in the apparel wholesale business as *bonak-dārs*; (2) those who have been working and learning business methods in the Tehran Bazaar as apprentices, and who, although not being shop owners themselves, have invested money in the purchase of Chinese goods in partnership with others; and (3) those who used to run apparel-producing firms or used to be workers in such firms. Attention should be paid to the fact that in all the three cases, the traders themselves go to China and purchase goods directly from the Chinese market. That said, some of those belonging to category 1, stopped going to China after a few purchasing journeys for a variety of reasons, including the belief that going to China does not help with the demand for goods in the shop or that the cost of travel is too high. Based on

[2]Some areas can be found in Tehran where franchises of famous foreign brands are beginning to gather. These include Mīrdāmād Street and Āfrīqā Street, both of which lie close to upmarket residential areas in the north of the city.

[3]Besides the Tehran Bazaar, shops selling cheap apparel products have also have appeared on Jomhūrī-ye Eslāmī Street.

information gained from the interviews, the main actors responsible for bringing Chinese goods into Iran belong to categories 2 and 3.

Traders who belong to category 2 are not necessarily people who are involved in the apparel business, and the amount of money invested by each individual is, in fact, quite small. Regarding joint investment groups of this kind, surveyed Informant FF, an established wholesaler in the Tehran Bazaar, remarked:

> In the old days, the merchants (*tājer*) brought the goods and *bonak-dār*s bought from them. The retailers bought from the *bonak-dār*s. People used to distribute goods in such a way… As for today, a few apprentices (*shāgerd*) of the Bazaar go into partnership (*sharīk*), contributing a matter of ten million tūmān each…courageously go to China…Even if a merchant has a capital of five billion (*tūmān*), it does not guarantee the success of his business anymore because these apprentices, say four boys, go over there, bring goods of about fifty million (*tūmān*) with them, and destroy the merchants' market.[4]

According to this view, fewer business opportunities now exist for conventional merchants who specialized in international trading since even newcomers with scant amounts of capital have been able to enter the import business without difficulty.

The traders who are perhaps most worthy of our interest are those belonging to category 3. Until only a few years ago, these producers used to make a sample of the product, which they would then use to produce versions by themselves, selling the products on commission in the *bonak-dār* clusters in the Tehran Bazaar or other places. But many of the merchant-producers in this category, in response to realizing how easy it was to purchase in China and the extraordinary cheapness of Chinese goods, closed down their own factories and engaged in the purchase of Chinese goods, thereby starting a new career as distributors. Their motive has been simple and straightforward: it costs much less to buy goods from China than to produce them independently.

A second fact relevant to the discussion is that in most cases, such traders go to China to purchase goods either individually or as members of small groups, relying on word-of-mouth information among their friends or in the Tehran Bazaar.

A survey respondent from Firm IR, who has been going to China for about four years to purchase goods, remarked:

> When I was tackling a lot of problems (concerning the apparel-producing business), a friend of mine took me to China. There I saw the things were cheap and I could buy them very easily. The profit was also considerable. So, I stopped production.[5]

Another Informant JZ, which is an ex-producer of apparel products and is currently engaged in the wholesale business in the Tehran Bazaar, emphasizes the ease of purchasing in China:

> Not at all (I had an acquaintance in China). I went on my own and went around asking people…Of course (I could carry out the purchasing) quite easily.[6]

---

[4]Interviewed on December 11, 2010.

[5]Interviewed on January 16, 2011.

[6]Interviewed on April 26, 2011.

None of these buyers, however, possess detailed knowledge of current circumstances in China, and hardly any of them can communicate in Chinese. Why are they able to purchase goods in China so easily despite their inexperience and lack of abundant capital? To answer this question, a unique feature of the supply side must be pointed out.

The cities that the buyers visit to make purchases are Guangzhou and Yiwu, both world-famous for their "Specialized Markets (zhuanye shichang)," which are sales centers of exportable manufactured commodities (such as daily goods and apparel products) in modern China. According to Ding, in China, many "Specialized Markets" have emerged next to industrial clusters, each one forming a trading cluster for a specific, usually locally produced item such as textiles, apparel, and mobile phones. These clusters would distribute products to secondary markets in various regions of China and, from there, to local consumer markets downstream in the trading network (Ding 2011). Some of these markets, such as the one in Yiwu, carry out a stronger collection and distribution function, dealing not only with local products but also with goods from other clusters both inside and outside the province (Ding 2008). Guangzhou and Yiwu resemble each other in that they each have a greatly expanded "Specialized Market," although each market has its own history and distinct pattern of location. Moreover, observers have pointed out that both markets in question offer a very advanced infrastructure for foreign buyers compared with other industrial clusters within China.

Iranian buyers are unanimous in saying that there is no difficulty involved in the purchase of goods in China. This is largely down to the strong existing infrastructure for foreign buyers, which consists chiefly of the following services. In China, buyers first visit one of the "interpreter-guide agencies" operated by Iranians (or Chinese), and the agent arranges an interpreter able to handle translations between Chinese and Persian or English. Iranian traders who have visited China say that these interpreters are all Chinese and some of them have even obtained some fluency in Persian while studying in Iran. In addition, interpreters for various non-Persian languages such as Arabic and Turkish are available. The buyer, accompanied by his interpreter, tours the clusters (buildings where the producing firms have offices for business negotiations and exhibit samples of products) and places his orders. In some cases, the buyer selects the goods from the samples offered while in other cases, the buyer shows a sample brought from Iran and asks the firm if they can reproduce it. The terms for delivery are generally short, rarely exceeding "a month at the longest." It is customary for some amount of deposit to be paid when the order is placed, and the outstanding balance is transferred to the firm's bank account after delivery. In principle, the relationship between Iranian buyer and Chinese firm ends at the conclusion of every transaction.

In some cases, Iranian buyers remain in China until the ordered products are ready; otherwise, they entrust an Iranian agent who lives in China with the final inspection of the finished products as well as with loading, dispatch of the goods, etc.

Some local companies supply a series of services systematically. For example, the Hopeful Trade Company, located in Yiwu city, offers a variety of services such as "sourcing, purchasing assistance, translating, warehousing and cargo inspection, logistics, documentation, expediting and all-time supervising, and customs clearance consultant." These are outlined in a pamphlet given to clients.

None of the Iranian buyers interviewed by the author expressed any anxiety over public security in China. Some say that when in China, they feel safe even when a problem with a transaction arises since everything is under the disciplined supervision of the police. Furthermore, they point out that many attractive extras can be gained by visiting China over and above their primary objective of purchasing products to take back to Iran. These include low commodity prices and a full range of amusements.

Perhaps the emergence of this kind of infrastructure has been particular to the "Specialized Markets" of Guangzhou and Yiwu, probably in response to the market's widespread adoption of a sales approach that targets foreign buyers, compared to other "Specialized Markets" in China. These helpful services on the supply side provide an infrastructure within which even Iranian buyers who have little information about China can purchase goods quite easily and cheaply.

Third, the interviews showed that other than China, both Turkey and Dubai were also considered worthy destinations by Iranian buyers. Informants pointed out that buyers who search for relatively expensive products go to Turkey while those who search for goods costing even less than in China travel to Dubai. Over the course of the interviews, it became clear that Dubai's markets play a collection and distribution function regarding cheap exports from Asia, including China. But in both Turkey and Dubai, buyers normally purchase finished products while in China, they are always able to arrange for a certain design to be produced in accordance with the demands of their customers. This is one of the reasons why China's "Specialized Markets" attract far more buyers.

Finally, the apparel products brought into Iran by the traveling traders are distributed all over the country through conventional sales networks such as the Tehran Bazaar. As already mentioned, the major clusters of *bonak-dār* shops that deal with foreign apparel products are located in the Tehran Bazaar. Some of the old-established trading clusters in the Tehran Bazaar, which were formerly known as places piling up cheap goods, are now supplying foreign goods as their stock in trade, shifting from goods made in Iran and catering to demand from domestic customers (namely, retailers and provincial wholesalers).

6.3 The Weakly Organized System as the Origin of Transition

We have seen recent changes taking place in Iran's apparel industry, changes that are reflected in the statistical data and the findings of the author's recent fieldwork. It is clear that Iran's apparel industry, which once nearly monopolized domestic demand, has undergone a sort of "liberalization" since the 2000s and has been subject to intense pressure by foreign products, including Chinese goods.

Instances of cheap Chinese goods, especially light industrial goods, sweeping across national markets elsewhere in the world are too numerous to mention; in that sense, Iran's apparel industry is by no means unique. This phenomenon, to put it plainly, owes much to the beneficial circumstances on the supply side. In the case under discussion, circumstances in China have been such that a large population inhabiting a vast territory has realized a comprehensive production system under protective policies by the government and the country is able to mass produce cheap products promptly. But if we look at the situation from Iran's side, the fact emerges that the immediate causes of the massive inflow of Chinese goods can be traced back to circumstances existing in the production and distribution system of Iran's apparel industry prior to import liberalization. Now let us consider such a sudden transformation occurred in the Iran's market for apparel products.

6.3.1 Rise of Newcomers

As stated in the first section, those who brought massive amounts of Chinese products into Iran's apparel market were none other than Iranian traders, especially those connected with the firms originally engaged in apparel-producing activity. With regard to the apparel industry, let us begin by considering how far market liberalization caused "changes of the actors within the distribution system."

After the 1979 Revolution, the import business in Iran was strictly controlled under the government's overall restrictive economic policies. Therefore, traders who were able to engage in the import business were very few and far between. During this period, the domestic distribution of apparel products was almost entirely monopolized by *bonak-dār*s, who held all domestic sales channels. Moreover, domestic distributors such as *bonak-dār*s specialized entirely in selling collected goods, drawing a clear distinction between their own role and that of international traders. These conditions prevailed until the relaxation of import restrictions in the early 2000s.

In general, when an import restriction is relaxed, we can normally expect an immediate increase in the number of traders with overseas links. However, in the case of Iran's apparel market where such traders did not exist before the early 2000s, the question arose as to who would engage in overseas trade.

At the outset, the author assumed the possibility of the following developments occurring. First, it seemed reasonable to expect the number of people with some sort of background in textiles and apparel importing would increase. Such people would include the above-mentioned *namāyande*s, some merchants who "bought" import quotas, and some producers to whom import quotas had been allocated in the past and so on. The fact that such individuals had the practical know-how about handling government permits seemed to support this assumption. Second, it might be surmised that some *bonak-dār*s might enter the import business in order to procure foreign goods to sell on themselves. Third, the number of foreign suppliers of goods might increase.

As stated earlier, however, since the early 2000s, the main actors in the massive inflow of foreign apparel products (mainly from China) were (1) joint investment groups consisting of apprentices in the Tehran Bazaar, (2) ex-owners or ex-employees of the apparel-producing firms in Iran, and (3) some *bonak-dār*s who had been engaged in apparel wholesaling for many years. This means that those who entered the import business after deregulation were not the established merchants who, in the past, had been involved in international trade (or had the appropriate trade know-how) under the existing distribution system but rather newcomers to the field.

It is worth noting that the goods brought in by newcomers from overseas were distributed all over the country through existing channels without any particular problem. It goes without saying that the *bonak-dār*s are able to sell foreign goods they purchase abroad in their own shops. Even the above-mentioned joint investment groups and former producers are also able to sell Chinese apparel easily in the domestic market.

Some special circumstances should be considered. First, the Iranian distribution system itself does not have as strong organizational barriers to entry as generally considered to be the case. In Bazaars that typify Iran's traditional marketplace, no limitations are introduced from the marketplace regarding the social qualifications and specialization of those who operate businesses there, nor are the origins of the goods that are brought in questioned. There is a "barrier" of sorts in the form of expensive rents stemming from the place's peculiarity, and a scarcity of shops exists. The trader only needs to secure the onerous right of using the place, a task bearing no relation to the route through which he brings the goods to the market.[7] The above-mentioned joint investment groups and ex-producers are able to sell the low-priced goods purchased in Guangzhou and Yiwu without any difficulty in the Tehran Bazaar, which is in that sense "an open market."

Another circumstance bearing consideration is that those who are involved in production activities demonstrate a high mobility between various business fields. As mentioned above, Iranian apparel-producing firms, most of which are non-organized independent firms in management terms, do not particularly continue to engage in only production activities as long as they are able to maintain operations as business entities. Since entry to the distribution field is comparatively easy, small-scale firms that have no accumulation of capital and/or skill come and go quite freely between the spheres of production and distribution. A former producer who goes to China to purchase goods told the author that his experience in production activities helps him to appraise goods in China's vast "Specialized Markets." In some cases, the Iranian buyer requires the Chinese firm to imprint their own logo on the product, which the buyer then sells in Iran. It is as though

[7]Some buyers seem to rent shops temporarily from someone who has *sar-qoflī* of the shops, and some sell the goods they purchased in China to existing merchants.

insignificant small-scale firms from Iran are moving their production bases abroad, remarking as they do so that they would like to reopen their factories if the domestic environment improves.

Such an elastic relationship between production and distribution, although comparatively unstable, functions as a safety valve for individual firms under Iran's "weakly organized" system where no vertical and horizontal relationships exist among firms.

6.3.2 *"Order Production" Realized by "Specialized Markets"*

Another important impact of "market liberalization" upon the weakly organized system of Iran's apparel industry was how it resulted in bringing the "order production" system to outside the country, a feature that had hardly developed inside Iran until then.

As has been repeatedly stated, conventional Iranian distributors had minimal direct connection with producers. The *bonak-dār*s' main business activities were limited to collecting finished products that the producing firms supplied and carrying out commission-based sales with the possibility of some return. *Bonak-dārs* were not involved in product planning at any stage.

On the other hand, the "newcomers" who visit China to purchase goods repeat the routine through which they found success in the "Specialized Markets" of Guangzhou and Yiwu. In other words, they check the samples, order products for sale in Iran, and await the delivery. The fact that this "order production" system—which was never used by distributors in the traditional apparel-producing scene—was realized so easily can be seen as epoch-making in the Iranian context. It needs to be pointed out, moreover, that this feature owes much to foreign goods-producing firms. To put it plainly, this means that China's "Specialized Markets" are remarkably superior to domestic producers (at least, Iranian buyers consider so) with respect to offering "a short period for delivery," "an immediate response," "few troubles at the time of payment," and the like. Iranian buyers' impressions regarding China can be seen from the following remark by Informant IR:

> There is no problem (for doing business in China)...It is a free and safe country for foreigners. Turkey is not as safe, for example. Although Turkey is nearer and I understand their language, I still think that China is much better.[8]

At the same time, the fact that no organizational relationship exists between producers and distributors inside Iran is one reason why production can be transferred offshore in a short time without any troubles over the entrenchment or merger of operations. The following is an interesting remark by Informant J2:

[8]Interviewed on January 16, 2011.

> I select the exhibitors that seem good (in a trade fair in China) and get the business cards and telephone numbers of the firms, then I make contact with the factories...sign the contract, pay the money, and discuss the date of delivery...I'm only engaged in order production. No one dares to set up a factory in China.[9]

Iranian buyers are not anxious to establish capital ties with Chinese firms on a long-term basis for producing their orders even in the "Specialized Markets." This may reflect the fact that the Chinese "Specialized Markets" are comprised of an enormous number of small-scale firms that can respond quickly in both producing and distributing to meet the needs of the numerous small-scale firms that survive under Iran's weakly organized system. This may suggest that a type of globalization initiated mainly by small-scale firms around the world is now underway and that this type of globalization differs considerably from that led by the advanced industrialized countries.

6.3.3 An Open Market in Production and Distribution

Let us now examine the ease with which production activities can readily be swapped with distribution activities taking into account the weakly organized system of Iran's apparel industry.

Under a weakly organized system, even in cases where each firm's capital is small (a fact that is true of the great majority of cases), few firms place themselves under the big capital's umbrella. In such circumstances, the accumulation and improvement of skills never occurs, and "specialization" is never developed.

At the same time, each firm's need to maintain business operations entirely by its own efforts means that firms tend to attach greater importance to diversifying business activities rather than specializing in a single business so as to disperse the risks inherent in every business. That is, an apparel-producing firm would tend to invest its surplus resources in businesses other than those related to apparel. As a consequence, the firm's concerns regarding the type and category of business, or even craftsmanship, are considerably weaker compared with manufacturing in Japan, for example. This inclination can also be observed in terms of personnel. In Iran, where firms operate independently, the production activity entails various risks. These include the challenge of personnel procurement—a problem that has been unanimously identified as a particular feature by those directly involved in the process. As firms generally assume that "workers do not stay long" or that "they no sooner learn skills than they set up businesses on their own," they are quite cautious from the outset about investing in personnel training or in expanding the firm. This corresponds with the fact that prior to the massive inflow of goods from China, few small-scale producer firms opened their own shops in the Tehran Bazaar. Iranian firms tend to prefer diversification of business management over the

[9]Interviewed on December11, 2010.

expansion of a particular business; therefore, a business operation that is engaged in both "production" and "distribution" of a particular commodity is almost unheard of.

Among the substantial number of small-scale firms that were secure as long as they faced only the limited competition in the "closed" market that prevailed under the government's import restriction policies, many were of course obliged to withdraw completely after the introduction of import liberalization. On the other hand, some firms that are keen to diversify their business but suffer from low accumulation of skills have chosen to enter the import business, avoiding the various pitfalls that accompany domestic production activity. Moreover, many of them remarked that they always have a realistic possibility of returning to production if conditions should change.

Incidentally, the top-ranking firms with more than 10 workers that have established their own brands are the ones who seem to have broadly welcomed the rapid increase in apparel imports. This might reflect the fact that the ensuing competition led to an improvement in product quality. These firms, which are involved in exports to Germany as well as to neighboring countries such as Iraq and Afghanistan, were originally eager to adopt quality control and introduce individual branding of their own products (Iwasaki 2012a, 15)

Both the long-established menswear producing Firm H[10] and the leading menswear producing Firm G2[11] affirmed that the inflow of foreign products had not influenced their markets. Nonetheless, it is clear that the inflow of foreign products, including European brands, came as a shock to high-ranking Iranian firms, a point reinforced by the fact that the number of firms having more than 10 workers shrank by 50% during the last 10 years. Nevertheless, aggregate output from this category has maintained previous levels. This indicates that the firms who have survived tough competition gained strength after import liberalization and expanded their overseas sales channels while maintaining market share at home.

Meanwhile, it is no wonder that the conventional merchants who possessed relatively more capital and the know-how for dealing in international trade most likely chose agency contracts with foreign high-class brands rather than purchasing cheap apparel goods with low profit margins. In the low-price and volume sales market, where even petty traders can procure goods and sell without much cost, merchants are highly unlikely to gain monopolistic profits.

It now becomes clear why the Iranian apparel market was "overwhelmed by Chinese goods." It can be due to Iran's weakly organized system but was also a phenomenon brought about by the existence of huge product-supply centers in the form of the Chinese "Specialized Markets." Attention should be paid to the fact that the "Specialized Markets" visited by Iranian buyers for purchasing are also "open places" where countless tiny producing firms are waiting for chance encounters with customers, hanging their samples in their shops and hoping for the

[10]Interviewed on August 17, 2009.

[11]Interviewed on November 14, 2010.

best. It is as if a series of production services are modularized and displayed for sale in the hope that spot transactions are made, if only just once. This fundamentally differs from the product-supply style common in retail trading in advanced industrialized countries, such as the organized process of securing market share and expansion of the market by distributors, the creation of medium- and long-term business relations, and the like. The Chinese system described here bears a remarkable resemblance to prototype forms of market trading and is in some ways recognizable in traditional marketplaces everywhere. In important ways, traditional market sellers and buyers get together in the same place at the same time and fulfill demand through competition at a particular point in time and space. The *bonak-dār* shop clusters in Iran are essentially of this type. The production and distribution system of this "marketplace" type may indicate, in short, a high affinity for the needs of firms operating under the weakly organized system like the Iranian one where no formal barriers to entry exist.

This point is not totally unrelated to the fact that the "Specialized Markets" that have developed in various regions in China currently attract not only large numbers of Iranian buyers but also traders from other so-called underdeveloped areas such as the Middle East, Africa, Central Asia, and South America. The argument in this study might serve as a demand-side answer to the question of why the "Specialized Markets" have that much drawing power.

References

Ding, K. (2008). Ichiba wa Naze Chūshō Kigyō Katsuyaku no Butai ni Narerunoka?: Zakka Sangyō ni miru Shinkō Shijō Baryūchēn no Sōshutsu Katei (An observation of the Process of Value Chain Creation in Emerging Markets from the Perspective of the Daily Necessities Industry). *Chūgoku Sangyō Kōdoka no Chōryū (Trends in Industrial Upgrading in China)* (pp. 179–206). Chiba: Institute of Developing Economies.

Ding, K. (2011). Chūgoku no Sangyō Hatten ni okeru Seisan, Ryūtsū Kankei:Sengyō Shijō Sisutemu no Shiten kara (The Relationship between Production and Distribution in the Industrial Development in China: From the viewpoint of Specialized Market System) http://www.ide.go.jp/Japanese/Publish/Download/Report/2010/pdf/2010_407_04.pdf

Directorate-General for Export-Import Regulations. (2004). *Export-Import Regulation Act 2004–2005*. Tehran.

Directorate-General for Export-Import Regulations. (2005). *Export-Import Regulation Act 2005–2006*. Tehran.

Directorate-General for Export-Import Regulations. (2006). *Export-Import Regulation Act 2006–2007*. Tehran.

Edāre-ye Koll-e Moqarrarāt-e Sāderāt o Vāredāt-e Vezārat-e Bāzargānī. (2000). *Moqarrarāt-e Sāderāt o Vāredāt va Jadāvel-e Zamīme-ye Ān, Sāl-e 1379 (Export-Import Regulations)*. Tehrān.

Edāre-ye Koll-e Moqarrarāt-e Sāderāt o Vāredāt-e Vezārat-e Bāzargānī. (2003). *Moqarrarāt-e Sāderāt o Vāredāt va Jadāvel-e Zamīme-ye Ān, Sāl-e 1382 (Export-Import Regulations)*. Tehrān.

Edāre-ye Koll-e Moqarrarāt-e Sāderāt o Vāredāt-e Vezārat-e Bāzargānī. (2004). *Moqarrarāt-e Sāderāt o Vāredāt va Jadāvel-e Zamīme-ye Ān, Sāl-e 1383 (Export-Import Regulations)*. Tehrān.

Edāre-ye Koll-e Moqarrarāt-e Sāderāt o Vāredāt-e Vezārat-e Bāzargānī. (2005). *Moqarrarāt-e Sāderāt o Vāredāt va Jadāvel-e Zamīme-ye Ān, Sāl-e 1384 (Export-Import Regulation).* Tehrān.

Iwasaki, Y. (2012a). The Business Management Strategy of Iran's Large Apparel Firms: Overview of Results from a Questionnaire Survey and Interviews 2009–2011. Discussion Paper No. 327. Institute of Developing Economies, Chiba.

Iwasaki, Y. (2012b). Globalization under a "low-organized" system: A case study on Iran's apparel industry. *Ajia Keizai (Asian Economy), 53*(5), 2–27.

Markaz-e Āmār-e Īrān. (1998). *Sāl-nāme-ye Āmārī-ye Keshvar 1375 (Iran Statistical Yearbook),* Tehrān.

Markaz-e Āmār-e Īrān. (2004). *Sāl-nāme-ye Āmārī-ye Keshvar 1382 (Iran Statistical Yearbook),* Tehrān.

Sāzmān-e Touse'e-ye Tejārat-e Īrān, Edāre-ye Koll-e Moqarrarāt-e Sāderāt o Vāredāt. (2011). *Moqarrarāt-e Sāderāt o Vāredāt-e Sāl-e 90 (Export-Import Regulations).* Tehrān.

Trade Promotion Organization of Iran, Directorate-General for Export-Import Regulations. (2008). *Export-Import Regulation Act 2008–2009.* Tehran.

Chapter 7
Conclusion

Abstract Under the weakly organized system of Iran's apparel industry, independent production firms concerned with maintaining their self-sustaining business employed special characteristics such as the *namāyande* system, *vizitōr* employment, and the distribution channel through the *bonak-dār*. This business style seems to have been an immediate cause for the massive inflow of Chinese products in the 2000s, together with the development of China's "Specialized Markets." As these markets are open to any purchaser, this enabled participation in this new market not only by Iranian conventional distributors but also by former producers who only quit that aspect to start new careers as "merchant." This nimble and prompt change of business activity from production to distribution originates in Iran's weakly organized system. As a result, a type of globalization has been realized between the two countries where the transactions conducted feature a "one-time-only" nature.

Keywords Weakly organized system · Self-reliant business style · Globalization · Marketplace type of a products-supply center

7.1 Self-reliant Business Style

The foregoing discussion has provided an examination into the industrial organization characteristics of Iran's apparel industry and the consequent massive inflow of Chinese goods into the Iranian apparel market since the early 2000s.

Over the course of the research, a model emerged of the typical Iranian apparel firm that persists in maintaining independence of operation regardless of firm size and which is inimical to the construction of long-lasting business relations with other firms—let alone vertical integration between firms—in all stages from production to distribution. In other words, it is a distinguishing feature of Iran's apparel industry that the relevant involved firms are barely organized compared to their counterparts in advanced industrialized countries. They operate in a weakly organized system where no vertical relationships exist among firms.

Y. Iwasaki, *Industrial Organization in Iran*, SpringerBriefs in Economics,
DOI 10.1007/978-981-10-4579-0_7

The circumstances in which countless tiny firms operate independently without becoming contractors of the larger firms or making contact with related distributors seem rather chaotic. An overarching organizer of production activities does not exist, nor does a sales promoter. Yet, the system has developed some specific practices that enable the firms to maintain their independent business.

One of these practices is the *namāyande* system used for the procurement of machinery and raw materials. The *namāyande* works as an agent upon the request of small-scale firms to find appropriate sellers who can meet these firms' demands. He also serves as a management consultant to small-scale private firms, collecting and analyzing information on the current business environment. This is a great benefit for firm owners who have limited time and capability for these tasks.

Interestingly enough, the relationship between a *namāyande* and clients is based totally on their personal ties. The *namāyande* bases his business on a relationship with the specific individual who owns the firm and never approaches his clients as a collective business organization. Firm owners also develop very close personal relationships to assure the safety of their business instead of relying on public or societal systems. They even seem to maintain these kinds of personal ties regardless of arising business opportunities. After the import liberalization of the 2000s, when the need for the *namāyande* shrunk considerably, the *namāyande* and his clients nevertheless remained in contact as if preparing for possible difficulties that might arise again in the future.

Another device for firm owners to maintain their self-supporting business is the distribution channel through the *bonak-dār*. A firm employs a person (or persons) called *vizitōr* to visit *bonak-dār*s' shops accompanied by products (or samples) as a deputy sales staff. The *bonak-dār* is not directly involved in goods' production, nor does he engage in any particular sales promotion activity. He displays the products collected in his shop, and if he reaches an agreement with a retailer or provincial wholesaler who visits the shop, he signs up. Without the agency of the *bonak-dār*s, producers would be hard pressed to open their own sales channels, let alone maintain them. The *bonak-dār*s's distributing function allows independent small-scale producing firms to operate their own businesses while selling the resulting products at very low volumes.

Here again, we can observe the non-collective ties that a *bonak-dār* has with his clients and business partners. The *bonak-dār*'s counterpart in every transaction is the individual firm owner (or nominee *vizitōr*) or buyer who drops by his shop. Each *bonak-dār* concludes a large number of contracts, but each contract is always on a person-to-person basis.

In this way, the self-supporting business style based on the weakly organized system of Iran's apparel industry extends into many related business activities. This structure, in fact, created the very opening for the massive and rapid inflow of Chinese products into the Iranian market after import liberalization while no collective counter-action was made by Iranian business people.

As stated at the beginning of this study, it is absolutely certain that a massive inflow of foreign (mainly Chinese) goods amounted to "a fierce attack from an Asian rising country" for Iran's domestic producers. If we examine the situation carefully, however, the Iranians seem to have sought a way out and have made positive use of the newly emerged opportunities to ensure the survival of their own businesses.

As mentioned earlier, not only conventional distributors but also producers shut down their factories and started new careers as distributors, relying upon word-of-mouth information to identify where cheaper goods could be found—goods that meet the consumers' taste. It rather indicates that people do not permanently possess a spirit of inquiry and passion for manufacturing but rather demonstrates these qualities only when the economic and social conditions so demand. The insignificance of the barrier between production and distribution in Iran originates in the fact that the entire industry comprises a weakly organized system. Under the circumstances the self-reliant firms tend to disperse the risks inherent in every business through diversifying business activities. As a consequence they rushed, avalanche-like, into selling cheaper foreign goods in order to survive as business entities.

The fact that the Iranian distribution system itself lacks strong organizational barriers to entry, even in the Tehran Bazaar, which typifies the traditional marketplace in Iran also accelerates the trend. No limitations are placed on entering the marketplace with regards to social qualifications and specialization for those who operate businesses there, nor are questions raised regarding the origins of the goods introduced, as long as one can afford the rental rates that reflect the marketplace peculiarity and the relative scarcity of shops.

7.2 Globalization of the Weakly Organized System

Meanwhile, an important feature emerged during the discussion. A kind of globalization is progressing where two weakly organized and relatively open systems in developing countries, namely those of Iran and China, have linked up with each other in a particular "place."

It needs to be noted, however, that each transaction has basically a "one-time-only" nature and thus these linkages are quite temporary and do not imply the development of permanent relations between the parties concerned. The Iranian buyers make casual visits to shops operating in the "Specialized Market" to purchase goods and do not think of building deeper business relations.

This type of globalization has, of course, been realized by today's tremendous improvements in the means of international transportation and communication. However, it should be affirmed that the system described herein has ancient origins because to a large extent, it adheres to the methods of market operation prevailing prior to the emergence of modern actors, such as the nation state and multinational companies, which so often serve as a framework for arguments regarding the nature of contemporary globalization. Attention also should be paid to the fact that the trend of so-called globalization exhibits interesting variety in both actors and the form it takes, a form that depends on the unique historical and cultural context of every country and region.

Finally, the author would like to indicate some points that may be worthy of future investigation, based on the argument professed in this study. Let us assume a case where the "marketplace" type of a sizeable and strong product-supply center like China's "Specialized Markets" no longer flexibly meet the needs of a weakly organized system. Even in present circumstances, a shift to vertical integration of firms, in the "industrialized-countries style," can be seen in China. Coincidentally, rising costs in China have begun to weaken the interest of Iranian and foreign buyers. In that case, what will satisfy the demand for the services currently offered by the "marketplace" type of products-supply centers? Are "places" with functions similar to those in China likely to come into being somewhere in the world other than China?

It will also be worth examining whether or not the reentry of Iranian buyers into production activities can, in fact, take place in cases where the "marketplace" type product-supply centers vanish. In such a scenario, will the weakly organized system be maintained or will a new order be introduced by actors such as multinational companies who have some degree of involvement in the production and distribution system inside Iran? These are among the many points of significance arising from the research.

Each of these points is closely related to the survival requirements of the weakly organized system itself. This study has not attempted to explain why the weakly organized system has endured so long in Iran's apparel industry. The fact that all of Iran's industries, including the apparel-producing industry, clearly share similar features suggests that the problem's essence is determined by an environment that is more extensive than might at first appear.

The survival of weakly organized industries may thus also stem from the state of management risk applying to all of Iran's businesses. The risk is not only related to a particular industry or item but also reflects the general weakness and arbitrariness of public infrastructure concerning the settlement of accounts and lawsuits. Moreover, the risk originates in the way people choose to behave based on such weaknesses and arbitrariness. Investigation of this aspect would need a stronger hypothesis with a good number of case studies and thus lies beyond the remit of this study. In this regard, comparative studies may provide useful insights into the apparel industry in other regions such as China and Vietnam, where the main production role is carried out by small-scale firms that are not yet fully "organized."

Index

Y. Iwasaki, *Industrial Organization in Iran*, SpringerBriefs in Economics,
DOI 10.1007/978-981-10-4579-0